MW01598712

Dear David,

Our conversations determine our results. This book lists out and shares some powerful conversational moves that can enable you to shift the results of your team.

Best wishes, Samir Dua

— Feb 2020

SAGE was founded in 1965 by Sara Miller McCune to support the dissemination of usable knowledge by publishing innovative and high-quality research and teaching content. Today, we publish over 900 journals, including those of more than 400 learned societies, more than 800 new books per year, and a growing range of library products including archives, data, case studies, reports, and video. SAGE remains majority-owned by our founder, and after Sara's lifetime will become owned by a charitable trust that secures our continued independence.

Los Angeles | London | New Delhi | Singapore | Washington DC | Melbourne

Advance Praise

Too many of us—leaders, managers, even youngsters—get trapped into the flow of the routine. In *Declaring Breakdowns*, Sameer Dua provides a how-to manual that—through examples and anecdotes, combined with a theoretical underpinning—presents a way out.

Highly recommended reading for anyone who wants to change their life and create a new future.

Kiran Karnik
Former President, NASSCOM

If you are looking to actively create a better future for yourself, a future of your choice, then this book is the tool to show you the way. Based on his experience in coaching as well as from his personal life, Sameer Dua nicely explains the 6-step process, from declaring a breakdown to executing the missing actions, to achieve the desired future.

A great read as well as a fantastic advisor!

Gerd Hoefner
Managing Director and CEO
Siemens Technology and Services Pvt. Ltd

Sameer introduces us to an interesting leadership move called 'declaring a breakdown'. Individuals, teams and organizations, all have a default future. Getting aware of this default future, and then creating a new future of choice, I believe, is a powerful leadership act. I see this move of declaring a breakdown as a new edge for the corporate world, and I would be delighted to see this new leadership move being actively used by leaders across different walks of life.

I love the fact that Sameer speaks about practice as a way to embody new learning. The 6 steps identified by Sameer in this book, when practised regularly, have the potential of transforming individual lives and organizations.

Tarun Katial
CEO, Reliance Broadcast Network

This book could not be more relevant for the current times. For a world that is changing very rapidly compared to yesteryears, Sameer's insights definitely deserve a read.

Tapan Singhel
Managing Director and CEO
Bajaj Allianz General Insurance Co. Ltd

Everything is possible. Even the word impossible says—I AM POSSIBLE.

This is exactly what Sameer Dua brings out in his book, which helps an individual declare a breakdown and identify the actions that need to be taken to achieve a desired future, which is completely different from the default future, using the 6-step process.

Negative sounding words such as 'breakdowns' and 'interruptions' have been projected in a completely different light, in this simple and practical book, which is a must-read for every individual leader. By quoting real-life instances, Sameer leads the readers by example.

One of those rare gems, *this book* is perfectly suited for both the corporate world and personal development.

Vandana Tanna
Country Manager and CFO
American International Group Inc. (AIG), India Liaison Office

In this book, Dua provides a strong 'how-to' for those who are ready to claim their agency and take a proactive stance towards creating a brighter future.

Veronica Olalla Love
Chief Executive Officer, Newfield Network, USA

The special gift Sameer has is reflected very much in this book. He enlightens the audience with certain truths that were hidden from them before, and raises the awareness of a leader to a whole new level. These ideas and practices can be used to significantly increase success and bring real results. Leaders can become what they can and want to be when they have this high level of awareness and some specific tools they can use.

Sameer's ideas are always pragmatic and clear, and at the same time inspiring. They demonstrate deep understanding of how humans—people—think and act, and the belief in people's ability to control their acts, their future and their leadership.

I enjoy reading Sameer's notes, as much as I enjoy listening to him talk about leadership in his seminars, which are always inspiring and mind openers.

Sharon Kedem-Shanny
Vice-President Delivery APAC, Amdocs

Sameer Dua has written a clear, no-nonsense, practical book that will help leaders lead. He has laid out and connected dozens of useful (and non-discretionary) distinctions that most leaders have never seen nor practised. He has presented his ideas with an engaging enthusiasm and passion that derive from his personal experience as a trainer and coach. I strongly recommend Sameer's book to any leader committed to improving his or her level of professionalism and effectiveness.

Dan Newby
Ontological Teacher, Coach and Mentor

After reading Sameer's book, 'breakdowns' can hardly continue to be seen as those 'problems' we continuously face and fight on a daily basis, consuming a lot of energy and resources in organizations, communities and our lives. Instead, they transform into great opportunities to design a different future, by changing the traditional approach to see them as 'enemies'. The book is clearly written and provides the readers with a useful, powerful and universal distinction to face the challenges that breakdowns usually bring with them. The 6 simple (yet not trivial) steps bring a beautiful simplicity to address this complex issue in a practical way.

I was enthralled in the reading from the very beginning with Sameer sharing his personal experience with breakdowns. The table of contents was like an exquisite menu of relevant conversations waiting to be opened. The generative practices at the end of each chapter are personal invitations for reflection and immediate action. Sameer leaves up to you, how far you want to go in the journey of creating a different future for your life, your family, your organization, your community, your country and the world.

Jose F. Rojas
Life Insurance Vice-President
Compañía de Seguros Bolívar
(Bolivar Life Insurance Company)
Columbia, South America

As a public school educator and leader for more than 30 years, I have been engaged for most of my life in an ongoing exploration of the importance, process and power of human learning. In this book, Sameer Dua shares an elegantly simple blueprint for navigating life events and circumstances, which might otherwise be impediments to learning and growth, in ways that expand the horizon of possibilities for creating and achieving a more desirable future in our personal and professional lives.

His explanations of different speech acts and conversation types and how these might be effectively integrated to generate new possibilities for action and living are clear and compelling, and the practices he offers to enhance the skills needed to declare and work through the breakdowns and challenges we face in life are highly appropriate.

If you are interested in exploring a different way of observing and 'showing up' in the world that results in new and exciting opportunities for learning and productivity, Sameer Dua's book is a 'must-read'!

Christopher S. Adams
Superintendent of Schools
Hempfield School District, Lancaster, Pennsylvania

Declaring breakdowns has astonishing possibilities for leaders of all organizations. I regularly see leaders of organizations get into a flow that they then find difficult to break out of. This book provides the knowledge and the practices to declare a break from the old flow and create a new flow.

Very few books help readers change their lives—this is one.

Tarun Sharma
Chief Customer Officer, APJ, BMC Software
CEO of BMC Software India Pvt. Ltd

Declaring breakdowns is a powerful concept introduced by Sameer Dua that many leaders may be subconsciously using. But doing this purposefully will take away the ambiguity and possible denials of breakdown, which may lead to a more powerful future state. The conversation style and examples make the issues come real.

Satish Nadiger
Managing Director and CEO (Country Manager)
John Deere India Pvt. Ltd

Declaring Breakdowns is a fascinating book by Sameer Dua. I pride myself on being a voracious reader but must confess that I have rarely come across a book which so lucidly takes you through a journey of rediscovery and gives you a deep insight into the immense potential which is locked down in a human being. We glibly talk about out-of-the box ideas and lateral thinking, but this book is one such gem which truly explains the rationale for the quest in our lives, our struggles, our relationships and ambitions from a very fresh perspective.

As an army officer, who has spent his entire life in the profession of arms and leadership as the mainstay of success, I found a book giving clear guidelines on how to rediscover alternates seamlessly as we get bogged in the routine and status quo. Sameer very persuasively opens your mind to the option of taking a deliberate pause when there is a slowdown or there is no light at the end of the tunnel to take stock and take the next fork. This considered and conscious breakdown he illustrates can be the catalyst for a better result in all your endeavours, whether personal, professional, organizational or even spiritual.

His writing style is very warm and compelling, and it seems like an interactive conversation rather than reading a great book. I could feel him across the table as I read through the book. His personal and humane qualities and social commitment to organ donation and just being a good human being shine through the book and touch your heart. My compliments and admiration to Sameer for putting this book out for people to read and introspect.

Lt Gen. Sudhir Sharma
Chairman, MitKat Advisory Services

DECLARING BREAKDOWNS

DECLARING BREAKDOWNS

Powerfully creating a future that
matters, through 6 simple steps

SAMEER DUA

www.sagepublishing.com

Los Angeles | London | New Delhi | Singapore | Washington DC | Melbourne

First published in 2016 by

SAGE Publications India Pvt Ltd
B1/I-1 Mohan Cooperative Industrial Area
Mathura Road, New Delhi 110 044, India
www.sagepub.in

SAGE Publications Inc
2455 Teller Road
Thousand Oaks, California 91320, USA

SAGE Publications Ltd
1 Oliver's Yard, 55 City Road
London EC1Y 1SP, United Kingdom

SAGE Publications Asia-Pacific Pte Ltd
3 Church Street
#10-04 Samsung Hub
Singapore 049483

Published by Vivek Mehra for SAGE Publications India Pvt Ltd, typeset in Adobe Caslon Pro 11/13 pts by Zaza Eunice, Hosur, Tamil Nadu, India and printed at Sai Print-o-Pack, New Delhi.

Third Printing 2017

Library of Congress Cataloging-in-Publication Data
Name: Dua, Sameer, author.
Title: Declaring breakdowns : powerfully creating a future that matters,
    through 6 simple steps / Sameer Dua.
Description: Thousand Oaks : SAGE Publications India Pvt Ltd, 2016. |
    Includes bibliographical references and index.
Identifiers: LCCN 2016001973| ISBN 9789351509837 (pbk. : alk. paper) |
    ISBN 9789351509844 (ebook) | ISBN 9789351509820 (epub)
Subjects: LCSH: Leadership. | Self-actualization (Psychology)
Classification: LCC HD57.7 .D823 2016 | DDC 650.1–dc23 LC record
    available at https://lccn.loc.gov/2016001973

ISBN: 978-93-515-0983-7 (PB)

The SAGE Team: Sachin Sharma, Sandhya Gola and Rajinder Kaur

This book is dedicated to my family, my strength:
Amma, Daddy, Mummy, Papa, Mamma, Shalini, Prashant, Rashmi
and Namrata.
My beautiful wife, Tina, and my three lovely children, Ashna,
Anaaya and Ayaan.

Bulk Sales

SAGE India offers special discounts
for purchase of books in bulk.
We also make available special imprints
and excerpts from our books on demand.

For orders and enquiries, write to us at

Marketing Department
SAGE Publications India Pvt Ltd
B1/I-1, Mohan Cooperative Industrial Area
Mathura Road, Post Bag 7
New Delhi 110044, India

E-mail us at **marketing@sagepub.in**

Get to know more about SAGE

Be invited to SAGE events, get on our mailing list.
Write today to **marketing@sagepub.in**

This book is also available as an e-book.

This book is for people who are committed to designing a future of choice; not for those who are committed to their excuses.

Contents

II. The 6-step Process at a Glance

List of Figures

Author's Note

I have been a student of generative leadership and am a coachee of Robert (Bob) Dunham, the founder of the Institute for Generative Leadership (IGL). In partnership with Bob Dunham, I have founded IGL in India. Bob is a generous man, and big-heartedly shares his knowledge with his students. Despite his very high standard of kindness, his generosity has had no limits when it comes to me. I am overwhelmed and humbled by Bob's love for me, for which I remain ever grateful.

What I want to admit to, right at the outset, is that much of what I have learnt about generative leadership is through Bob Dunham and IGL. I have referred to Bob's papers at several occasions in this book, and in many cases, I admit, I may not have referenced these effectively, only because I have referred to my notes of the many papers of Bob and IGL.

This book would not have been possible without Bob's support and the use of his papers. He has also graced this book with a foreword, and like most of his writing, I invite you to read this foreword like you are having a conversation with Bob, relishing and soaking out the juice of every sentence.

To ensure confidentiality of my coaching clients/consulting clients, I have either only referred to their industry or changed names of individuals. In certain cases, so that it is not obvious to employees in certain organizations, I have changed the example a little bit but retained the core point from that coaching.

Sameer Dua
Founder and CEO
Institute for Generative Leadership, India

Foreword

Failure is simply the opportunity to begin again, this time more intelligently.

—Henry Ford, American industrialist and Founder of Ford Motor Co.

The wise words of Henry Ford have strongly resonated with me throughout my journey from a young entrepreneur without any business experience to the globe's 100 most influential people in the field of medicine. At each stage of this long and arduous journey, I have been beset with failures. And each time I failed, I have bounced back stronger than before. My journey has been about leadership without worrying about failure and the challenges along the way. It has been about determined leadership to succeed. It has been about not giving up. It has been about not taking no for an answer.

When I look back at my journey, I realize that unbeknownst I was, as Sameer Dua describes in this book, 'declaring breakdowns', at every crucial juncture of my life and in doing so creating inflection points. I was, as this thought-provoking book explains, actively participating in my life by being in the process of creating or designing a future of my choice.

This book has a refreshing take on breakdowns. In fact, it shatters the norms and the lens through which we normally look at breakdowns. It introduces breakdowns as a practice of declaration for the sake of creating a future of choice. I believe, from the leadership perspective, the next big thing after disruptive thinking would be to actively 'declare breakdowns'.

I quite like the point Sameer has made in his book that each individual, each project, each team, each organization, each country has a default future; a future that is probable, and yet almost certain. And that most of us are blind to this default future. This plain awareness of the default future is an invitation to us to create a new future of choice. In hindsight, I can clearly see the number of times my default future was not so appealing to me, and each time that happened, I created a new future and took persistent actions to achieve that future.

For example, when I did not get admission in a medical college due to my grades, I initially experienced defeat. However, I did not allow these internal conversations that created the experience of defeat to brew for long. I changed my conversations with myself, and got committed to my new future.

Inside of my commitment, and my love for science, I chose to study BSc (Hons) in Zoology with chemistry and botany as minors. I studied hard to excel and got the first rank in the university. It was my own little way of saying to these colleges, 'Look at what you missed out on—I could have been a good doctor.' I declared a breakdown and designed a future of my choice, rather than exist in drift.

Then again, after I graduated, in a conversation with my father, my future changed. My father drew my attention to the science of brewing and helped me create a future in the world of brewing. At that time, brewing was a fairly nascent stream in India and there were not many professional brewers. There were cultural assessments that stopped women from working in this male-dominated industry. I never accepted these cultural assessments, challenged them, created my own new assessments, and because of this, I proved myself in a vocation yet unexplored by Indians and more so by women the world over.

I could identify with Sameer's 6-step process of declaring breakdowns completely as I see how I have been working on those steps in my life. I have always been cognizant of the present in terms of where I am, and very clear on where I want to go (my future of choice), and have accordingly focused on what actions I need to take today, to get to where I want to go.

At the very outset in this book, Sameer talks about how conversations change our world. The deeper you go in this book, the more you realize the importance of conversations in the matter of achieving results and success. I can clearly see how my conversations with myself, my conversations with my colleagues, the conversations my colleagues have with each other, the conversations we have with our customers—each of these conversations—impact the results of my organization.

The book suggests that breakdowns do not exist by and of themselves; they are brought into existence by us and that when we declare breakdowns, we take responsibility, that is, we are the cause in the matter of achieving the result that we have declared. I find this concept ground breaking and significant. Any result can be achieved, as long as people take the posture of 'I will cause that result—come what may.'

In fact, what Sameer does through this book seems to find resonance in another field that he is passionately engaged with— organ donation.

As a founder of the Gift Your Organ Foundation, Sameer's efforts have helped raise awareness for the need to voluntarily pledge our organs so that those can be harvested after our deaths to save several other lives.

As an activist, Sameer asks you to act on gifting a better future to another person. As an author, he invites you to act on creating a better future for yourself.

In providing the reader with the knowledge of how to declare breakdowns and the platform to get skilled in declaring and dealing with breakdowns effectively, this book focuses on generating action, and thereby results.

Remember, life does not always pan out exactly the way you thought it would. Yet, you *always* have the power to redesign your future and create breakthroughs in your life.

I believe to succeed in life one needs to inculcate a spirit of challenge and a deep sense of purpose. I started out with the ambition to be a doctor, but as a researcher and an entrepreneur, I have been able to touch many more lives.

I invite you to this wonderful journey initiated by Sameer and to engage in practices he has elucidated at the end of each chapter. Remember, results are a function of action—you cannot be sitting on the sidelines and hoping for results to come automatically. Similarly, to get skilled in leadership, you have to participate in leadership practices, and one such key practice is the practice of declaring breakdowns.

Kiran Mazumdar Shaw
Chairperson and Managing Director
Biocon Limited

Foreword

I met Sameer Dua in 2013 at a coaching conference where I had made a short presentation about coaching in organizations. I had founded IGL in the USA in 1993, and he informed me that, independently and without knowing about me, he had recently founded an organization which he named IGL in India. Clearly, we needed to get to know each other!

We are co-travellers on a similar journey. We have since become affiliated companies and draw from the same heritage and foundations of thought and practice. This core tradition is called 'ontology' and was begun by Fernando Flores in the early 1980s, and has been developing in a number of directions since then, including our work in 'generative' leadership and practice. We both study the work of my friend Julio Olalla, who founded the ontological coaching, as well as many other threads of unfolding discourses in the world that contribute to our mission to enable people to discover, develop and harness their capacities to create and realize a future that they care about.

There is an extraordinary moment that many of us experience in our lives, a moment of awakening and new illumination that shows us a new world. Our lives are never the same after that moment, as it touches the deepest part of our being and provokes a sense of profound possibility and aliveness. It is sometimes referred to as an epiphany, a paradigm shift or a crucial moment of inflection in our life paths. Both Sameer and I had experienced such moments in our learning journeys, and we decided that sharing this experience and making it a practical and powerful part of people's everyday life would be our life's work.

Sameer's invitation in *Declaring Breakdowns* is an invitation to discover your own capacity to change your future, the future you share with others, and to make it happen. He provides an extraordinary set of simple steps that empower us to break through our usual limits, fears and comfort zones to embrace our birthright to create our lives rather than drift in them, or suffer from them. What is powerful about this simple, but not trivial, practice is that it has the ability to match any scope of concern we may bring, from shifting our team meetings to be more effective or managing our time better to the quality of our relationships, enhancing our professional skills, creating a future where we fulfil our dreams or making a significant impact in the world.

This is possible because our innate make-up as human beings has a capacity to create—to create our thoughts, emotions and sensibilities, as well as our commitments, interactions with others, cares and actions. We can, and already do, create who we are, who we are becoming and how we impact others and the world. The problem is that most of us do not know that, may not believe it or do not know how.

How we see our world and act in it, including how we see ourselves, is a product of history: our own personal history and the history of our families and cultures in which we grow up. History shapes the kind of human being we are, and that shape is captured in our bodies, emotions, language, practices, perceptions and interpretations. We see what we see, but we are also blind to what we do not see. Illuminating this blindness is part of the journey of unleashing our innate power to create.

In history, we see the process of illumination. There was a time when people thought the world was flat, and then a new interpretation illuminated the world in a new way. There was a time where alchemy was our best knowledge about the dynamics of the world, and then physics and chemistry produced a new kind of illumination. The world did not change, but the interpretations in which we see the world did change.

We also see illumination in our own personal histories, as we learn our habits and behaviours in our families, schools and experiences.

We enter career paths, and we enrich our lives through learning in fields of our interests. But for most of us, this learning happens in an old historical interpretation of what learning and education are. As a culture, we are only recently beginning to question and see a different kind of learning, a different kind of illumination and a different context. In this new context, we illuminate new fundamental aspects of being human, of how we create our futures, how we take actions, where we stop ourselves and where we break through. Not as some unexplained and unusual experience for a rare few, but as a path of learning available to anyone. We go beyond understanding concepts to experientially learning about ourselves, about our relationship with life and the world, about our possibilities and how we can shift our actions, habits and impact in the world.

This new path of learning has been illuminated by new perspectives from the research and advances in many fields, including neuroscience, linguistics, cognition, emotional intelligence, high performance, biology of embodied learning and ontological studies, and new applications in leadership as well as organizational design and practice. What is fundamental to all of these advances is that they are newly illuminating how we become the human being that we are and how we can guide our learning and becoming so that we can become our best as the person and leader we want to be. We are not confined to repeat our past. We can be the creators of new futures.

This kind of learning cannot be done by only understanding new concepts. It requires the learning where we see our world differently, we act in it differently, we understand and sense it differently, we behave differently, we have different skills and habits and we are more clear and connected to what we care about and what we are committed to. This is the learning to become more of yourself, rather than learning more things to know and do.

This learning requires embodied learning, to actually shift ourselves through practice. The study of mastery, practice, habits and high performance has revealed how this is done, and how to meet the challenges along the way. This is the kind of learning being made available to you in *Declaring Breakdowns*.

What is fundamental to declaring breakdowns as a skill and practice is that you see that you have the innate power to intervene in the drift of your life, to respond to any interruption of the flow of your life and to create inflection points to a new future at any moment. This is literally available to all of us. Yet we have generally not learnt that this is possible, nor have we learnt how to do it. You will learn this in this book, if you are willing to take the simple steps of the path.

We can always be too busy to learn. We can always return to our comfort zone rather than make something powerful happen. We can always relax into our drift rather than design and create. Or we can take the stand that we will author our lives, we will act to take care of what we care about, that we will go from drift to design, we will develop our power to create and we will take responsibility to create our future with others rather than have the stories of why we cannot.

The choice is ours. It is always there. You are invited to take the next step, just one small step, and then the next one, and so on, creating your future and the journey of your life.

Robert (Bob) Dunham
Founder
Institute for Generative Leadership, USA

Acknowledgements

I began working in September 1992 and spent 20 years running management institutions in India and the UK. I first came across ontology, *the study of beingness*, when I attended Landmark Education programmes, and these programmes created enough impact and curiosity in me to want to discover more. That led me to Newfield Network and then IGL, USA. I continue to be actively involved with IGL, and this book is a result of the impact that the programmes of these institutions have had in my life.

It is important to state that several different giants in the field of ontology have already stated much of what is written in this book. This book is an endeavour to use their work and share in my voice this powerful leadership move of declaring breakdowns. While this book may be built on the work of several leaders, the interpretations are mine, and I take responsibility for the divergence.

While writing this book, I stand in complete acknowledgement of the outstanding work of thinkers such as Martin Heidegger, John Austin, Dr Fernando Flores, Werner Erhard, Julio Olalla, Robert (Bob) Dunham and many more who I cannot possibly name.

I have had the privilege of being a student of Newfield Network and directly learn from Julio Olalla. As Henry Adams stated, 'a teacher affects eternity; he can never tell where his influence stops'. Julio has impacted my eternity, and his influence continues to enhance my life.

At Landmark Education, I studied under several programme leaders and coaches. However, Dr Viji, the programme leader for the Self-Expression and Leadership Program (SELP), deserves a special mention. My London enterprise was going through liquidation and my family life was distraught while I was her student. She taught me the real meaning of 'responsibility' and that changed the course of my life!

Sunil Jain, then a programme leader in the making at Landmark Education, coached me on several occasions, and those coaching sessions transformed the way I looked at life. Today, he is a dear friend and among the most powerful men I have ever encountered in my life. Despite his disability, he is the epitome of someone who always has a choice in every single moment of his life. I continue to learn from every interaction that I have with him.

For the last 5 years, I have had and continue to have several coaches who have played an important role in my life. I am grateful for their contributions in my life.

Kiran Mazumdar Shaw, a leading businesswoman in Asia, the chairperson of Biocon and the chairperson of the Governing Council of the Indian Institute of Management Bangalore has written a foreword for this book. She is the brand ambassador and has actively supported the Gift Your Organ Foundation, an NGO that I co-founded in 2010. I am not too sure if she knows how much value just her name has in India/Asia. I am delighted that she took out time to go through my book and share her views through her foreword.

Before I sent this book to publishers, I requested several of my friends to review this book and provide their feedback and comments. This book has been enriched by comments from Jagdish Chawla, Daniel Newby, Pam Fox Rollin, Newell Eaton, Sailaja Manacha and, particularly, Dr Christopher Adams and Bob Dunham—both of whom spent significant time on the book and gave me detailed paragraph-wise comments.

This book is my first publication, and I am appreciative of the support of Sachin Sharma and SAGE. Thank you for trusting in me and my work, and I do believe we have a long way to go together. I look forward to going on this journey with you.

A special acknowledgement to my dear friend Sheeja Shaju. She has been a colleague at IGL, India, ever since it began in 2013 and is my partner for life in this journey. I would have given up this book a long time ago had it not been for Sheeja. She has supported me in many ways in the writing of this book. Her commitment to this book, our organization, our programme participants and humanity, in general, inspires me. I remain indebted to Sheeja for her love and compassion.

I am also thankful to my other colleagues at IGL, India, for their exceptional support and commitment to the organization, and to me personally. This goes out especially to Dhanashree, Shilpa and Joe.

I have 2 heroes in my life who I have not mentioned yet. These are guys I have grown up watching and wanting to emulate all my life. These heroes are my father and my brother, Prashant. Both of them have always kept my interest before theirs, promoted me, encouraged me, cheered me and ensured they always take the fall, while I have a soft landing. My fearless and bold attitude comes from the fact that I know I have these heroes to reach out to, should I ever need something.

And above all, it took me 12 years to really start to 'listen to' the love, the selflessness and the hard work my wife, Tina, puts in ensuring that I have great comfort in my life. She takes exceptional care of some of our key cares—our family, our home and our beautiful children, creating an uncluttered space for me to write this book and to go out in the world and do my work. I love you.

And, finally and most importantly, I thank you—the reader— for picking up this book to read. I hope you enjoy reading it.

Preface: The 5 AM Club

I was leaving Bengaluru in February 2012, after my wife and my daughter left me on 31 August 2011. I was returning back to Pune, which was home. My wife moved back to her parents' place, which was also in Pune; my then company was headquartered in Pune; and my parents also lived in Pune. I had all the reasons to return home to Pune.

The one concern that I had was that my entire structure, a group of friends I had come to trust, who held me together and saw me as who I was—'a possibility', lived in Bengaluru. I feared that once I moved back to Pune, I would lose touch with them and then they would not be available to support me.

Before I left Bengaluru, I met two of my friends, Jerry and Dinesh, over dinner. This concern was constantly on my mind, and I wanted to do something about this. Over dinner, I shared this concern with Jerry and Dinesh. What ensued was an interesting conversation and resulted in the creation of what we called 'The 5 AM Club'.

We invited 4 other friends, Rajesh, Priyanka Shylendra, Saju Joseph and Sumit Gupta,[1] in addition to Jerry, Dinesh and myself—and the 7 of us formed The 5 AM Club.

All of us connected on a conference call at 5 AM every morning. The calls lasted between 20 and 25 minutes.

We began The 5 AM Club:

1. Each one of us identified our important cares or the different areas of our life that mattered to us.
   I identified the following areas that I cared for:

   • My family

- Gift Your Organ Foundation
- My organization and the growth of my organization
- My personal development

2. Once we had identified what we cared for, we declared a future in each of these areas. We asked ourselves in each area of our care, 'One year from now, on this date, where would I like to be?'

3. The next question we asked ourselves was, 'So that I get to where I want to be 1 year from now, where will I need to be 3 months from now, 6 months from now and 9 months from now?'

Once we had declared our future of 3 months, 6 months, 9 months and 1 year, we asked ourselves, every morning, 'To achieve this future, what is it that I need to achieve today so that I achieve the future that I have declared?'

The following morning, the group would ask the other person whether they had indeed achieved what they had declared. The group provided support to individuals and acted as the structure for fulfilling the future that each one of us had created.

Interestingly, the following were the extraordinary achievements of individuals in The 5 AM Club:

1. Jerry Martin doubled his salary in 4 months.

2. Saju Joseph wanted to move with his family to the USA, and he did so. Today, he works as a senior executive in one of the largest IT companies in the world.

3. Priyanka Shylendra, as the Director Operations of the Gift Your Organ Foundation, declared that she would work with the Karnataka government and offer organ donation as a part of the driver's license form. She achieved this in 4 months from the start of the club. The impact with this one move was that the Gift Your Organ Foundation had 7 times more pledges in 6 months than what the Karnataka government had in 7 years. In 6 months, the number of organ transplantations that took place in Karnataka doubled from what had happened in the previous full year. The Karnataka

government acknowledged Gift Your Organ Foundation for their contributions.

4. Sumit Gupta started his own company in an area of his passion—cricket.

5. Rajesh, a wheelchair-bound person, a dear friend and my coach, declared that he would buy a red Hyundai i10 within 3 months. Let me bring some context here—Rajesh does not belong to a rich family. He had to work hard to get to where he has reached. When he declared he will get a red Hyundai i10, he did not know how he would do this (remember, he is wheelchair-bound and his legs do not function). Only once he made the declaration, he identified agencies in Europe that manufactured equipment for cars for the differently-abled. He imported that equipment and requested Hyundai to fit the equipment into the car.

Personally, I had some huge successes too. As I had mentioned earlier, my wife and daughter had walked out on me. I declared a breakdown and created a future stating that, come what may, I would get my wife and daughter back in my life. Not only did they come back in my life, after 20 months of separation, my wife and I have become parents of twins since. So, we now are a family of 5 with 3 children.

I sold my last organization and set up a new company, in the area of generative leadership. Gift Your Organ Foundation, a charitable trust that a friend and colleague, Tina Budhrani, and I had set up, has seen many highs since too. I have completed a series of new learning programmes and continue to be enrolled in one programme in the area of generative leadership inside of my commitment to my personal development.

Why am I sharing this with you?

The reason I am sharing this is because these are prime examples of what it means to 'declare breakdowns and create a future of choice'. Everyone in The 5 AM Club created a future—a future of design.

The questions that we asked—such as '1 year from now, on this date, where would I be?' or 'What is it that I need to achieve today so that I achieve the future that I have declared?'—are not routine questions that people ask themselves regularly. They force you to 'create where you want to be' and 'what you should do today if you want to achieve the future you have created'.

I have been running IGL in India for over 3 years and have invited hundreds of participants of my programmes to declare breakdowns in areas of their care and design new futures of choice. These distinctions have worked not only for the members of The 5 AM Club but also for my programme participants who have achieved new futures of design.

PART I
Getting Started

1

Introduction

I want to begin with a claim that declaring a breakdown is not a bad thing to do. On the contrary, it is a good thing to do. A very good thing to do. That is exactly what all of us in The 5 AM Club did.

When you declare a breakdown, you actively participate in your life, in the process of creating or designing a future of your choice. This book is about you getting skilled in designing a future of your choice. And to do that, you declare breakdowns.

One of the definitions of 'breakdown' in the dictionary is

the act of disrupting an established order so it fails to continue.[1]

Humans are most times blind to how and when a certain order gets formed and then we do not even question this order. This order is the way we do things. At a lot of times, this order works for us. And at many other occasions, we simply continue to operate in this automatic or programmed mode without questioning the order that gets formed. This now does not work for us anymore.

The way to deal with this is to declare a breakdown.

When I use the word 'breakdown', a lot of people 'listen'[2] to a mechanical breakdown. In one of my consulting assignments with a global organization with a turnover in excess of $40 billion—a member of the top management team laughed when I suggested that they declare a breakdown. He looked at the other members of the top management team and laughingly said, 'We declare breakdowns when the lift is not working or the printer is not working'. Later, when he understood the importance of declaring breakdowns, he said, 'This is so powerful! I'm surprised—I did not know this!'

This is the cultural blindness of today's corporate world. Many executives across the world do not know when and how to declare a breakdown. According to them, common sense states that you do not declare breakdowns. As a matter of fact, Bert Lance, the Director of the Office of Management and Budget in Jimmy Carter's administration, was quoted in the newsletter of the US Chamber of Commerce, Nation's Business, May 1977, stating, 'If it ain't broke, don't fix it'.[3]

While Bert Lance's claim does make sense in a lot of occasions, there are as many other occasions where it is prudent and makes business sense to declare breakdowns. There are hundreds of thousands of examples of businesses having closed down or gone into liquidation and a lot of these could have been saved, only if the relevant people within these organizations had declared a breakdown at the right time. Similarly, people would have saved their jobs; negotiators would have got the deals or contracts; teams would have completed their projects on schedule; and marriages would have been saved, if timely breakdowns were declared.

This book is an invitation to you to be aware of the almost certain, probable, default future (it is almost certain to happen, and yet is only probable).[4] Each of us, in each area of our life, has an almost certain, probable, default future.

Is this future acceptable to you?

If not, then this book extends the invitation to you to actively create a future of your choice.

A Breakdown to Be Declared

At this stage, in the introduction chapter itself, I want to declare a breakdown.

1. *What is the breakdown that I am declaring?*
   The breakdown that I want to declare is that there are only very few people who understand the need and the importance of declaring a breakdown. This book reconstructs the meaning of the word 'breakdown', from the existing cultural understanding of the word.
2. *What is so?*
   'What is so' describes the facts around the concerned issue. If you were to take a camera and go into boardrooms of organizations or meetings conducted by senior managers and middle or junior managers, the camera would capture how people are 'indulging' in problems, refusing to solve these problems proactively and engaging in a game of blame.
3. *What is the default future?*
   If no action is taken in this area, executives, senior managers and middle and junior managers will continue to act the way they are acting. Despite their 'best' efforts to serve the organization, their actions will not serve the organization, and as a matter of fact may even be counterproductive.
4. *What is the new future that I am creating?*
   The new future that I am creating, right now, is that these executives, senior managers and middle and junior managers understand how to declare breakdowns and the importance of declaring breakdowns, and actively declare breakdowns. Declaring breakdowns will be a commonly used leadership move. Leaders and managers will engage consciously in the process of creating futures that work for them and for their organizations.
5. *What is missing today for that to begin happening?*
   People are not declaring breakdowns simply because they do not know that they do not know. If they knew that they do not know, some of them would make attempts to learn. But when they do not know that they do not know—they are operating in 'blindness', that is, a state of no choice. What is missing is the understanding and, more importantly, the skill of declaring breakdowns. And for them to

get this understanding and skill, what is missing is an offer to them.

6. *Taking action/execution*

   This book is an offer to executives, senior managers and middle and junior managers. It is an offer to anyone interested in a life of design, rather than a life of drift. I am, in the process of writing this book, taking the action and bringing into execution what I believe is a great need of the hour for the corporate world (and for people's personal lives).

   However, the key action now is that you learn how to declare breakdowns through the concepts and practices provided in this book.

What I have just done is followed a simple 6-step process in declaring a breakdown. Once I have declared the breakdown, I am managing the breakdown by identifying and then taking the missing actions.

This simple 6-step process is what this book is about. If you believe you are skilled in declaring breakdowns after having seen the process shown above, you can safely stop reading the book here.

However, if you do not have the knowledge or if you think you have this knowledge and not the skill of declaring breakdowns, then I strongly recommend that you continue reading this book. Our claim is that knowledge is of no use if you do not know how to use the knowledge, and for knowledge to be useful, you need to practise.

Through this book, I am sharing simple steps to creating a future of choice by declaring a breakdown. Through this book, I am also offering simple yet powerful generative practices to follow so that you can engage in embodied learning of important leadership distinctions. Just because I call these practices simple, it does not in any way make these practices trivial. These are integral to your learning.

Getting a breakthrough means getting a big and dramatic success, and not incremental success. My claim is—declaring a breakdown is your access to creating a breakthrough in your life.

Who Is This Book For?

When you read this book, you will see me jump from personal examples of my coachees, to professional work-related examples of other coachees. I have also brought in a lot of my own examples from my personal life and also my work life. So, the question that may come up for you is, 'Is this a book for results in a reader's personal life, or to make one effective at work?'

This book has been written for anyone who wants to take care of what he or she cares for. What you may care for may be in the domain of your personal life, or in the domain of your work life. It is for leaders of teams, managers of groups of people, department heads, heads of functions and also for heads of organizations.

What is of importance is that you first know what you (as an individual, as a member of a team or an organization) care for, and then take care of what you care for. In my coaching work, there is a wide repertoire of examples that I could use, but I have intentionally brought in some personal examples shared by my executive coachees, because in that point of time, this is what my coachees cared for, and was of concern to them. The distinctions remain the same, irrespective of the domain of your life. It is important for you to acknowledge that you are at the source of your personal life and your work/professional life. This book is about you powerfully creating a future that matters—to you!

This book is for you if you are really committed to designing a future of your choice. This book is *not* for you if you are committed to your excuses.

A Suggested Approach for This Book

I may have not met you and may never meet you personally (although I would love to). However, through this book, I would like to have a conversation with you, I would like to share with you some integral distinctions of leadership, of declaring breakdowns and of creating a future of choice.

My request to you is to read this book as if you and I were engaging in a one-on-one conversation. The other request that I have is when you read examples of others, see yourself in those shoes—make these examples personal.

Please participate with me in this conversation with an open mind, ready and accessible to receive some new distinctions.

If you follow the above-mentioned methods, I am certain you will enjoy reading the book, and get immense value from it.

The Promise of the Book

This book invites you to your power, including your power of creating and realizing futures that you care about. The promise of this book is to provide the knowledge of how to declare breakdowns and the platform to get skilled in declaring and dealing with breakdowns effectively—through the practices elucidated in the later chapters.

In addition, this book will give you an insight into several generative leadership distinctions that, when practised, have the potential of having a significant positive impact on your performance. You can only get skilled by 'doing' the practices over and over again.

My request to you is not to read this book as some book to get done with, but one that provokes you, stimulates you, arouses you to go into the depths of your reflection. Please engage with the practices elucidated at the end of each chapter. My guess is if you pick up this book after 6 months, what did not seem relevant 6 months ago will seem relevant 6 months later.

This book also suggests several pauses for reflection. Please do stop and reflect on these questions. The real value of this book will not be in the reading of it; the real, juicy value of this book will be in you stopping and engaging with what gets provoked for you in the questions asked in this book. This book is about your life and living, not about information to remember, understand or to agree with or not.

What Is Learning?

The general understanding held by many is that you learn by knowing. There is a common myth and a cultural blindness that understanding something cognitively is the same as 'knowing it' or 'having learned it'. Learning, true learning, means to shift embodiment (what our body can see, attend, do and experience habitually), to shift the capacity for action and to shift what outcomes can be produced and promised. Learning is not just understanding, and is not only academic. By understanding the concepts in this book, you will only 'know about' how to declare breakdowns. However, for you to 'know' how to declare breakdowns, you will need to actively practise the distinctions provided in this book. There is a difference in 'knowing about' and in 'knowing', and the difference is practice. This distinction was made by the ancient Greeks, but has been forgotten in our current common sense of learning and education. Many of us, very often, confuse 'knowing about' with 'knowing'.

Learning is a function of regular practices that allow us to embody new skills and to act in new ways. By merely reading books, watching CDs or hearing audio tapes, you do not learn to embody new ways of being. What is required is to create new practices and take new actions.

Let us take the example of swimming (you can take driving, cycling, speaking in front of an audience, IT skills, conversing, managing teams or any other skill). If I gave you a book on 'How to learn swimming in 10 days', would you be in a position to learn swimming in 10 days? Obviously not. To learn swimming, you need to get into water and practise the concepts of swimming. In a classroom, or by reading a book, you will only *learn about* swimming, you will not *learn* swimming.

Similarly, this book does not intend to make you more knowledgeable with information, which is not my endeavour. The objective of this book is to strive to make you skilled in declaring breakdowns and in the 6-step process of creating a future that matters. To get skilled, you will need to 'do' what the book recommends you to 'do' at the end of chapters and in between chapters. And the more you do (practise), the more skilled you will get in declaring and managing breakdowns effectively. And by doing so, you will increase your capacity to choose the future you want and to make it happen.

What is learning?
Learning is to shift embodiment, to shift capacity for action and to shift what outcomes can be produced and promised.

What is not learning?
Learning is not just understanding, and is not only academic.

How does learning happen?
Learning happens through action and through practices. By understanding the concepts in this book, you will only *know about* how to declare breakdowns. However, for you to *know* how to declare breakdowns, you will need to actively practice the distinctions provided in this book. There is a difference in 'knowing about' and in 'knowing', and the difference is practice.

Reflective Pause

1. What has learning meant for you till now?
2. How is this understanding of learning different from your earlier understanding?
3. What new learning (through practice) have you recently undertaken?

Summary and Reconstruction Section in Each Chapter

After each chapter, there is a section called 'Summary and Reconstruction'. In each chapter, there are some important distinctions that have been reconstructed, and to highlight these distinctions, I have included them in the summary section of each chapter. These reconstructed distinctions are generative interpretations of common words that are used in English language. With these new interpretations, you get an opportunity to 'see' these distinctions differently, apply them easily and generate new practices as indicated in the Generative Practices.

The entire body of IGL work is based on 'generative' distinctions and interpretations, which means that we are dealing not just with concepts, models and conceptual frameworks but with behaviours that produce the desired results as well. To be generative, an interpretation must

- be observable,
- be executable,
- be learnable through practice and
- generate the desired result.

This book will provide conceptual understanding of the distinctions. However, conceptual understanding is just the starting point. There must be an embodiment of new skills, and for that we have also included a section titled 'Generative Practices' at the end of each chapter.

What Is a Generative Practice?

A generative practice is a conscious choice to embody a behaviour that can be used in whatever situation we find ourselves in. It is a commitment to a way of being in the world. It is life affirming, creative, and it produces a reality by how we orient to our life situation.[5] For example, a practice of 'listening' to the care of another is a generative practice (we will discuss more on this in Chapter 9).

Learning to type, on the other hand, is a specific practice; it is specific to a certain context and takes care of a specific concern. But typing is useful only when we are typing.

We can use a generative practice anytime, anyplace, for example, even when we are learning to type. When you are typing a letter, you can 'listen' for the care of the person you are writing to, and in your letter, you can take care of how the other person will receive your letter.

Generative practices come from a generative stance in life. We see that it is possible, and we take the stand that we can generate in any situation. We can generate our outlook, our emotional experience, our connection to care, our connection with others, the action we take and invite others to take, our conversations that open new possibilities, actions and results. Human beings are generative beings, but we have forgotten that. We are recovering our self-awareness and power that life has already given us.

Summary and Reconstruction of Our Understanding

1. Declaring breakdowns is a leadership move that not many know of. When you declare breakdowns, you author the future of your life and/or actively co-author the future of your teams and organizations. You actively participate in your life by being in the process of creating or designing a future of your choice.

2. This book does not treat learning as just understanding or only as academic. It treats learning as shifting embodiment, as increasing our capacity for action, and shifting what outcomes we can promise and what we can produce.

3. Learning happens through action and through practices. By understanding the concepts in this book, you will only 'know about' how to declare breakdowns. However, for you to 'know' how to declare breakdowns, you will need to actively practise the distinctions provided in this book. There is a difference in 'knowing about' and in 'knowing', and the difference is practice.

4. A generative practice is a practice that you consciously choose so that you can embody a behaviour (i.e., become skilful with it) which can be used in whatever situation you find yourself in. It is a commitment to a way of being in the world.

Generative Practices

1. You are always in some practice or the other. Write down what practices you have embodied, such that you are now unaware of its existence in your embodiment. For example, the way you sit in a meeting; your first reaction when you receive negative feedback or news; your tone and your language when you interact with your subordinates, or your family; the way you draft your emails; and your daily practices when you arrive at your office.

2. We discussed in this chapter that learning is a function of practices. What new leadership skills would you like to learn? To do so, create new practices, and schedule them in your calendar.

3. Start a practice of writing a journal. Record reflections of your practices in your journal. The purpose of the journal is not to fill it, but to hone our attention to observe ourselves, to observe others and to observe life more powerfully. Use this practice to provoke your being a better observer of how life happens for you.

   When you journal, you enter into a conversation with yourself. And like in a conversation with another person, you do not know what will come out of that conversation; similarly, when you begin to journal, you do not know what reflections you will end up creating in that conversation with yourself.

   I have found journaling to be a powerful practice, and I invite you to a daily practice of journaling—for the sake of your own leadership.

Notes

1. http://www.thefreedictionary.com/breakdown, accessed 16 February 2016.
2. There is a difference between hearing and listening. Hearing is a biological phenomenon, and listening is a linguistic phenomenon. To listen is to interpret what you hear. You can also listen to what you smell, what you see and what you feel.
3. http://en.wikipedia.org/wiki/Bert_Lance, accessed 16 February 2016.
4. I heard this phrase in a programme that I attended at Landmark Education.
5. Richard Strozzi-Heckler, *The Leadership Dojo: Build Your Foundation as an Exemplary Leader* (California: Frog Ltd, 2007).

2
The Centrality of Conversations

Effective conversations are central to declaring breakdowns, to designing a future of choice, to leadership and to living a good life. The first 5 of the 6 steps elucidated in this book are conversational (or generative) moves that we invite you to learn and master. These steps are not discretionary; they are a structure of human action that is required to produce new futures. Successful leaders follow these steps—even if they are not aware of the distinction of declaring a breakdown.

Breakdowns are declared and managed in conversations. To really get the power of declaring breakdowns, we need to reconstruct the term 'conversation', understand the power of conversations and distinguish generative conversations.

What Does 'Conversation' Mean?

The common-sense understanding of a conversation is speaking and hearing. Most people presume beyond speaking and hearing, there is not much going on in a conversation. This understanding of conversation is grossly inadequate. If we use the etymology *con* + *versa* from Latin, meaning 'to go together' or to 'change together', it would imply that in a true conversation, 'we move together to a new understanding'. Conversations are not just 'descriptive', but also have the power to create and generate.

I am presenting now a new way of understanding conversations.

Conversation is the interaction of human beings that creates action, meaning, listening, moods and emotions, connection with others and the future.

Conversations are not just words, but the whole body reactions that are provoked when we interact in language and when we interact and language is provoked.

Conversations include language, moods and emotions, body reactions and experiences and the listening that is based on the history of the people in the conversation. Conversations are shaped in linguistic and cultural practices.[1]

Let us unpack this distinction of 'conversation':

- *Conversation is the interaction of human beings.* Indeed. And each participant has a unique 'listening' of a conversation.
- *Conversations create action.* Some conversations create action. The source of all action is in some conversation or the other, a conversation one has with himself or herself or a conversation one has with another. For example, when I make a request or an offer to you, and you accept the request or the offer—we have a promise or a commitment. Once we have a promise, the future changes. The execution that you do in the future will have a great deal to do with the promises/commitments that you have made.

   Renowned French philosopher Jean-Paul Sartre is quoted to have stated, 'Commitment is an act, not a word'. Making trustworthy commitments and soliciting trustworthy commitments from others are missing skills in the world today.
- *Conversations create meaning.* When you speak, you bring meaning into something where there was no meaning earlier. For example, John tells Peter, 'This is a long and a boring meeting'. There was a meeting taking place—that is all there was. John, in his conversation, added his meaning

to the meeting, stating this is 'long' and 'boring'. John added that meaning of 'long' and 'boring'.

- *Conversations create listening.* When a conversation is on between 2 people, there are actually 3 conversations going on. For example, A and B are in a conversation. There is one conversation between A and B; the other conversation is the one that A is having with himself or herself, while in conversation with B; and, the third conversation is the one that B is having with himself or herself while in conversation with A.

  So, if A says, 'Your target for the last quarter was not met', B hears A say, 'Your target for the last quarter was not met', but 'listens' to the same statement as 'you are inefficient'. Now B responds to A not based on what he or she heard, but based on what he or she 'listened'.

- *Conversations create moods and emotions.* When the boss says, 'You are fired', this statement creates an emotion of 'anger' or 'sadness' or 'resentment' or maybe even 'relief'.

- *Conversations create the future.* When a meeting is set up for 2 PM on Thursday, or a summer vacation planned, a future is getting created. When a President of an organization articulates his vision for the organization, he is creating the future of the organization in conversation.

- *Conversations are not just words, but the whole body reactions that are provoked when we interact in language....* The bodies of individuals are in conversation, not just their heads. And hence you see bodies responding automatically to statements made by people. When a person receives a bad news, the body reacts with a particular churning in the stomach; similarly, when someone says something that touches you, you feel goosebumps.

- *... and when we interact and language is provoked.* When you interact with another person, and that person says something—what that person says provokes a particular listening in you. For example, Alex calls James and tells him that he cannot come for the weekly meeting of partners. This statement of Alex provokes an internal conversation in James that, for example, states, 'Alex is undependable'.

- *Conversations include language, moods and emotions, body reactions and experiences.…* Conversations are not just had in language. A conversation is the coherence of language, emotions and moods, body reactions and experiences.

  - I can say 'thank you' in a mood of gratitude, or the same words in sarcasm, or in anger, or out of frustration, or in any number of other moods. What the other person 'listens' will depend on not only what is said but also how it is said.

  - I can say 'thank you' in a body that shows I am in gratitude (with a smile, folded hands), or say the same words of 'thank you' with facial expressions that show 'I do not mean to say thank you, I am just saying it for the sake of saying it', or my facial expressions show sarcasm (a smirk). So, it is not only 'what' is said, and 'how' it is said—what matters is also in what body was it said—what were the facial expressions, what were the hand movements and so on.

  - I can 'say' thank you—without even saying thank you, with just a smile and a nod of my head—and it will communicate that I said thank you to him or her with gratitude.

The above-mentioned three examples indicate that conversation is not only the act of saying 'thank you' but also includes in what emotion are the words said, and the corresponding bodily actions, and these determine how the other person receives what you intend to communicate.

I am hoping with the earlier examples, you will start to see that conversations are the coherence of your language, emotions and the body. Each dimension always affects the others, and we cannot understand an experience without this coherence.

- … *and the listening that is based on the history of the people in the conversation.* All of us human beings bring our history in every conversation. The way we 'listen' to a conversation has a great deal to do with our history and our past experiences.

For example, in a workshop, what the programme leader says is the same for all. However, each participant 'listens' differently based on his past experiences and his history. When the manager gives a seemingly tough assignment, one employee 'listens' to it as 'the manager is trying to prove a point against me', and another 'listens' to it as 'what an opportunity'.

• *Conversations are shaped in linguistic and cultural practices.* How people listen to you has a great deal to do with their cultural practices. Fundamental differences among people arise from nationality, ethnicity as well as family background and individual experiences. These differences affect beliefs, practices and behaviour and also influence our expectations of one another. Here are some examples[2]:

- Family is defined differently by different cultures.
- Eye contact varies by culture. Children from many Latin American and Asian cultures show respect by avoiding the glance of authority figures.
- Physical distance during social interactions varies by culture. In areas of the Middle East and South America, people stand very close when talking.
- European Americans like to have more distance between them, while some African Americans prefer even more space. You can create great discomfort by standing too close to another person. Not being aware of this can even prevent someone from understanding or accepting the ideas you are trying to get across.
- Culture greatly influences attitudes about physical contact, whether it is a handshake, hug or pat on the back. In Asia, female friends often hold hands and men casually embrace one another as they walk down the street. Americans, however, may feel uncomfortable with such public behaviour. In some Asian cultures, affectionately patting an adult's head is strictly taboo, although it can be acceptable behaviour between adults and young children.

- Different cultures regulate the display of emotion differently. Some cultures get very emotional when they are debating an issue. They yell, they cry, they exhibit their anger, fear, frustration and other feelings openly. Other cultures try to keep their emotions hidden, exhibiting or sharing only the 'rational' or factual aspects of the situation.
- Cultures may use different standards for loudness, speed of delivery, silence, attentiveness and time to respond to another's point.

Conversation also takes the form of a dialogue in which there is an exchange of ideas, thoughts, opinions, suggestions, declarations and so on.

We have conversations to make sense of things, gain mutual understanding, create visions of possible futures, plan opportunities, coordinate action and deal with what is concerning us.

Conversations can be

- 'generative' when the focus is on telling a story, or creating a future;
- 'descriptive' when the focus is on describing;
- 'speculative' when the intention is to explore possibilities to clarify who we want to be or what we want to do; or
- 'active' where we create a mood for action so we can make and keep promises to each other to get a result.

What Does Conversation Mean?

"Conversation is the interaction of human beings that creates *action, meaning, listening, moods and emotions* and the *future*.

Conversations are not just words, but the whole body reactions that are provoked when we interact in language and when we interact and language is provoked.

Conversations include *language, moods and emotions, body reactions and experiences* and the listening that is based on the history of the people in the conversation. Conversations are shaped in linguistic and cultural practices."

Generative Conversations

Our common-sense understanding tends to be that communica-tion is to describe things, not generate them; we tend to believe that communication is simply for transfer of information, with an emphasis on good presentation rather than listening skills. What we are blind to or unaware of is that our language is generative. With language, we generate or bring things into existence.

Lera Boroditsky, a cognitive scientist from Stanford University, states:

> Do the languages we speak shape the way we see the world, the way we think, and the way we live our lives...? For a long time, the idea that language might shape thought was considered at best untestable and more often simply wrong.... What we have learned is that people who speak different languages do indeed think differently and that even flukes of grammar can profoundly affect how we see the world. Language is a uniquely human gift, central to our experience of being human. Appreciating its role in constructing our mental lives brings us one step closer to understanding the very nature of humanity.[3]

According to Zaffron and Logan,[4] 'generative language has the power to create new futures, to craft vision, and to eliminate the blinders that are preventing people from seeing possibilities. It doesn't describe how a situation occurs; it transforms how it occurs. It does this by rewriting the future'.

One way that language is understood in our current age is as a description of our world, a set of labels that we use to describe things and people, a medium for the transfer of information. Much research in language has worked in this framework—that words correspond to entities and phenomena in the world. We see that a word like 'chair' corresponds to an artefact by that name in the world.

This perspective hides that *language is generative*, not just descriptive. Language has the power to generate

- action,
- outcomes of action,

- possibilities,
- commitments,
- identities,
- opinions and much more.

Language is generative in addition to being descriptive. In this book, we focus on the aspects of language and communication that generate action, and thereby results; generate possibilities, meaning, value and satisfaction for ourselves and others; and even generate moods and emotions in our experience.

In the 1940s, philosopher John Austin at Oxford pointed out that we perform acts in language that are not descriptive, but that generate commitments and the future. He discovered that when we make a promise, for example, we are not describing something in the world. Instead, we are making an act, and the act is one of commitment—showing what the speaker is committed to—for the future. A request is a similar act, in which we do not describe something, but we make an act that shifts the future through the commitment that is spoken, listened and asked for. Austin called these linguistic acts 'speech acts'.

Bob Dunham expanded the speech acts to listening acts and stated that 'every speaking produces a listening in a listener. Speech Acts become Listening Acts when they show up in the interpretation of the listener. Listening is shaped by the history, standards, culture, practices, and the interpretations of the listener'.[5] So, it is actually the listening act that becomes more important than the speaking. It is what is listened that matters, rather than what is spoken.

Summary and Reconstruction of Our Understanding

1. If declaring breakdowns is a generative conversational move, and leadership is about having effective conversations, it is important to understand what 'conversation' means.

   Conversation is the interaction of human beings that creates action, meaning, listening, moods and emotions and the future.

Conversations are not just words, but the whole body reactions that are provoked when we interact in language and when we interact and language is provoked.

Conversations include language, moods and emotions, body reactions and experiences and the listening that is based on the history of the people in the conversation. Conversations are shaped in linguistic and cultural practices.

2. Our common understanding of language is that language is descriptive, a medium to describe, express, communicate or transfer information. This understanding of language makes people blind to the generative power of language. Language is also generative and creative, and has the power to generate actions, outcomes of actions, possibilities, meaning, commitments, identities, opinions and much more.

3. The key aspect to understand, in the context of this book, is that declaring breakdowns is a generative act, done as a powerful conversational move in language. You bring into existence, through your speaking, a breakdown, and use language to take the next missing actions to perhaps create a breakthrough. You connect to your power to create.

Generative Practices

1. In conversations with people,

    a. notice what people 'listen' may be different from what you actually intend to convey.

    b. notice what you 'listen' may be different from what people actually intend to convey.

    Start to become aware how you and others may be *listening to respond*, rather than *listening to understand* what the other is saying. We will develop this concept and practise as we go along.

2. Observe how you and others bring history and experiences into a conversation. Please observe how we *listen* has a great deal to do with our history, our culture, our experiences and our practices. Consider if you had a different history, cultural background, experience or practices, how would you have 'listened' to the same conversation.

3. Become aware of how your conversations provoke emotions in other people, and similarly, how these conversations provoke emotion in you.

4. Choose an emotion, for example, 'enthusiasm', and have a conversation in this emotion with someone. See the impact your conversation 'in enthusiasm' has on them and on you. Choose another emotion, let us say 'gratitude', and have the next conversation with this emotion. See the impact your conversation 'in gratitude' has on them and on you. Notice how you can choose an emotion, and each time you choose a different emotion, the conversation itself and its impact on you and the other person is different.

5. Listen for how conversations create the future. For example, 'Let's meet for lunch on Friday at 1 PM' changes what Friday 1 PM would have been like had you not requested for this lunch. The future changed when the other accepted your request. Observe how your future is getting changed in conversations—conversations that you have, and conversations that you do not have (you wanted to invite a client for a meal, but you did not make that request—you were hoping for a future where you would have that lunch, but because you did not have the conversation, your future did not get created).

6. Make a daily entry in your journal of the above-mentioned practices. Remember, journaling is engaging in a conversation with yourself. This conversation with yourself will help you clarify and acknowledge what you are experiencing, learning and what is relevant for you.

Notes

1. This distinction of 'conversation' has been created for IGL by Bob Dunham.
2. These cultural differences examples have been taken from Anne Arundel County, Maryland. http://www.aacounty.org/Partnership/Resources/Cultural_Differences.pdf, accessed March 2015.
3. Max Brockman, *What's Next? Dispatches on the Future of Science: Original Essays from a New Generation of Scientists* (USA: Vintage Books, 2009)
4. Steve Zaffron and Dave Logan, *The Three Laws of Performance: Rewriting the Future of Your Organization and Your Life* (San Francisco: Jossey-Bass/Wiley/ Times Group Books, 2009).
5. Bob Dunham's sessions in 'Coaching Excellence in Organizations' programme.

3
Transparency

Introduction

According to *Oxford Dictionaries*, the word 'transparent' means 'functioning of a process without the user being aware of its presence'.[1]

In our normal day-to-day lives, we humans are used to our routines. We are not aware of or we do not need to consciously focus on a lot of things that help us achieve results. These are the things that are transparent to us. They are sitting in our subconscious mind and do not demand our focused attention all the time.

Charles Duhigg, in his book *The Power of Habit*, states, 'one paper published by a Duke University researcher in 2006 found that more than 40 per cent of the actions people performed each day weren't actually decisions, but habits'.[2]

Our cortex, the site of consciousness, can process sensory input at about 40 events per second; in contrast, our limbic system, the site of our unconsciousness, can process about 20 million events per second.[3] Conscious thinking is mostly serial; unconscious thinking is mostly parallel. The body, therefore, moves our practices from conscious to unconscious performance so that they can be done faster and better.[4]

The unconscious performance of the body, or our habitual actions, is a great example of what is transparent to us. What is transparent to us does not mean it is not happening. It is happening and yet is transparent to us. We are not aware of it. We do not have our attention on it.

There are other meanings of the word 'transparent', and these are 'easy to perceive or detect', 'easily seen through', 'open', 'frank', 'candid' and so on. I am not using these meanings of the word 'transparent'. I am using the meaning of the word 'transparent' like as if there was a glass door to a store and a customer would walk right into the door without realizing the door was there. That glass door was always there; it was just transparent to the customer. Similarly, there are various aspects of our life that are transparent to us. They exist, but like the glass door, we miss seeing these, unless we pay attention there.

Transparency of the Present

As living beings, we breathe, yet we are not aware of our breathing all the time unless we specifically and consciously divert our attention towards it. We wake up in the morning and get up from our beds. Several parts of our body help in the process of alighting from the bed. We do not transfer our attention to these parts of our body. We just get up and go about our day. All the parts of our body that help us move are transparent to us.

Scientists say, as humans, we blink our eyelids on an average about 25,000 times a day.[5] In the process of blinking, our eyelids and our eyes are totally transparent to us. We are not consciously aware of their existence during that process of blinking.

Right now as you are reading this book, the function and contribution of your eyes towards enriching your experience of reading and their uninterrupted performance that keeps you reading are totally transparent to you until this very moment when I have diverted your attention to the action of you reading this page.

My 9-year-old daughter and I have had several conversations on conserving water, a depleting natural resource.

A few weeks back, one evening when she was brushing her teeth, she put on the tap in her washroom at full force. I could hear in the living room, where I was seated, the force of the tap in her bathroom, which is at one far end of our house.

When she walked out to say good night to me, I reminded her of our conversations on conserving water. She said, 'Of course, I remember, Dad! I do everything to conserve water.'

She was not lying—it is just that it was transparent to her that she had put the tap on in full force. Her attention was on her thoughts in that moment, and her 'present' (*tap flowing in full force*) was transparent to her.

There is a lot going on in every moment. Our attention is usually focused on a single matter or on a few matters at best. The rest is all transparent to us.

The World You See

For the fish, the entire world is under water. My assumption is that they do not even know that there is a world outside of water. The fish are incapable of coming out and searching for a new world. And hence, for them to believe that the entire world is under water may be acceptable.

However, as human beings, we have no such limitation.

And yet, we end up believing that the world we observe is the way the world is. We are caught up in *our own worlds*, that is, the world we observe, such that we do not even know that we do not know that there is a world beyond the one that we manifest. Every individual has a world, or worlds, that is different than anyone else's. This provides the power and richness of diversity, culture and possibility when we begin to share our worlds.

One of the dictionary meanings of the word 'world' is 'an area or sphere considered as a complete environment'. I draw from this definition when I say 'our own world'. We consider our realm as a complete environment. Like my assumption of the fish considering their physical underwater realm to be the complete environment.

However, our realm is not a *real* underwater world. Our world is made up of our own assessments, our judgements and our answers to questions. We form our own worlds, our own viewpoints, and then guard these so much that no one can challenge these. In other words, most of us now do not have an assessment; the assessment has gotten hold of us!

In a recent learning conference that I was leading, a director of a business unit of a leading German multinational corporation stated to me:

> I can see that my assessment is just that, an assessment, and not the truth. However, while I understand this conceptually, I am finding it difficult to drop this assessment. I can also see how this assessment of mine is restricting me in taking new actions. Despite that, I am finding it difficult to drop this assessment. It's like dropping a part of me which I have held as the truth for so many years.

This is what I mean when I state, 'most of us now do not have an assessment; the assessment has gotten hold of us' (we will discuss assessments in greater detail later in Chapter 6).

To get a better understanding of this, think of two people who work in the same organization (preferably your own organization). One person may be resentful and resigned in the organization, while the other is excited and charged up in the same organization. Both of them are living in the same physical world of 'what is so', yet both of them are living in completely different linguistic worlds of 'what they make of what is so'.

Linguistic world means the world you create in your language, most times subconsciously. The linguistic world that you live in is the world of your assessments, your stories, your judgements and your conclusions. It is like being a fish under water that refuses to acknowledge the other world out there.

However, the difference is, this linguistic world of your assessment is your creation, that is, the *realm that we consider as the complete environment.*

We will discuss 'assessments' in greater detail in Chapter 6.

A Short Exercise

I am going to ask you a simple question that will take only a few seconds to answer. My request to you is to respond to this question. As simple as it may seem to you, it has the potential to show something to you that you may have been blind to until now. Please respond to this question immediately on reading it.

So, here it is:

Look around you and find all 'green' that you see in the room. Try and find as much green as you can in the first 10 seconds.

Please do the exercise now.

Questions for you:

a. Did you find new 'green' in this room that you had not noticed earlier?
b. While looking for green, did you see any other colour?

There was a middle-aged lady who worked in a Singapore-based organization that I recently consulted to. She was convinced that her colleagues, including her seniors and her peers, were out to get her. (*This is what I mean by the 'world you live in'.*) She *lived* in this world where she believed people did not like her and wanted her to leave the organization.

In one of my informal lunch conversations with her, I did the same brief exercise with her, as given above.

I asked her to look around the cafeteria and identify everything that was green in colour. With an initial look of question, she jumped into the exercise and started to point me to all the green she saw: the artificial plant, the colour of the tiffin carrier of one of the employees of her company, the green line on the lampshade, a green checked shirt worn by a passer-by, some green design on the coffee machine on the counter, and so on and so forth.

I then asked her the following same two questions I asked you:

1. Had she noticed these green things before I asked her to look for the green in the room?
   Her response was 'no'.
2. Did she notice any other colour when she went out looking for green?
   Again her answer was 'no'.

Why do you think she (or if you did the exercise, even you) found green?

She (and you) found green because you went looking for it.

The invitation of this exercise was for you to see that *you get what you look for*. It is as simple as that.

This lady had all this while been looking for the 'green', that is, evidence that her colleagues were out to get her. And guess what she found! She found the green—every small action was considered to be evidence that she was not required in the office. She 'missed' all other evidence that suggested otherwise, the same way that she (and maybe some of you) 'missed' seeing other colours while she went looking for the green.

I left that lunch meeting asking her to now look for a 'new green'—that is, the greatness in her colleagues. I requested her to go all out looking for their greatness in every one. And when you go out looking for the green, you fail to notice any other colours. To cut the story short, initially, she had trouble doing so; however, with a little practice, she only found greatness in people, at work and everywhere else. She did not pay attention to anything else, or missed what did not point to the greatness of people.

So, here is a new claim:

The world you see is a function of the observer you are.[6]

And this is transparent to you. The common-sense understanding is—*the world* is *the way I see the world*.

According to Zaffron and Dave,[7] 'None of us see things as they are. We see how things occur to us'. We interpret what we see, based on our biases, our beliefs, our personal history, our culture, our moods and our practices.

Let me give you an example:

A coachee of mine had great relationships with most people she worked with or even interacted with. There was just one lady in her client organization that she could not get along with. Her justification to me (and most importantly to herself) was 'I work well with all other people. It is only with this person that I have a problem'. The unsaid in this was that 'the problem is with her, and not with me'.

It was transparent to her that every time this client lady's name came up, her body would tighten up. She took her assessment of this lady being unreasonable with her in every conversation, and guess what she found. The green! She found the unreasonableness in this lady.

I invited her to consider (*so that she could start to observe*) that *she was at the source of this relationship issue* with this client lady. We are at the source of what we pay attention to, what we emphasize, what possibilities we hold open or closed and what actions we are willing to take or not. We can hold a relationship as 'it is this way, it will not change and I will act based on this interpretation', or we can hold it as 'I see the relationship initially in one way, there are other ways, and I can take action to shift how I see it, experience it and how it plays out in interaction'.

> When you observe that you are at the source of how a particular relationship is, or for that matter you are at the source of any result that you currently have, you in effect give yourself the power to transform that relationship or that result.

This is a context shifting way of looking at life and is very powerful. When people blame others, they literally give away power to cause a shift to the other person.

This was transparent to my coachee. But the moment she observed the situation in this way, that she was at the source of this relationship not working, and that it was her who kept looking for the unreasonableness in this lady, new actions emerged for her— actions that were not available to her prior to our conversation. She started to 'look for' reasonableness, giving her the benefit of doubt. Very soon, she realized that this lady was actually much better than she gave her credit. She also saw new ways to interact with her, to produce a different result.

The way the world occurs to a CEO of an organization is different from the way the world occurs to a front-line employee of the same organization. The physical world 'out there' is the same. It is the linguistic world of interpretations and assessments of the two that differs (see Figure 3.1).

Reflective Pause

Take a deep breath and get aware that you have been breathing all this while.

Look around you and notice things that are kept in your room, that which you did not notice earlier. Notice life around you, in your room, outside the window/door from where you are sitting.

Now, turn your attention to your feet touching the ground (and if they are not touching the ground, feel the bed, sofa or whatever else they are touching). Feel the sensation in your feet. Move your attention to your clothes touching your body. Feel the sensation of your clothes touching the body.

All of this, and a lot more, was going on while you were reading this book. These sensations were transparent to you while you were in the flow of reading this book.

A question for you to consider—'What else maybe transparent to you as you go about leading your life?'

Please take a moment to reflect on this.

Transparency of the Future

I briefly referred to the almost certain, probable future in the Introduction chapter. I referred to this as the default future. This default future, while it is almost certain—is transparent to you. It is not in your conscious awareness that your actions or your inactions

Figure 3.1   The Two Worlds That You Live In

The *Physical World* that you live in	The *World* that you *Manifest*
One world is the physical world that you live in.	The other world is the world that you manifest. You also live in this world like you live in the physical world.
This world is the same for all living beings.	You are the only person living in this world. This world is exclusive to you.
You describe this world.	You create this world (in your thinking and speaking).
In describing the world, you are talking about what's 'out there'.	In creating the world, you reveal the way you see.
Here, the world comes first and then you describe the world with your words.	Here, the word comes first and then the world gets created (you speak and it gets created).
Your moods and emotions do not impact this world.	Your moods and emotions greatly impact this world.
This world is 'THE Truth'	This world is 'YOUR Truth'
This world does not impact your being-ness (all of us live in this world and yet all of us are 'being' different).	This world that you create, is the cause of the way you be.
In this moment, this is the way this world is, and you have no choice in how it is.	Here, you have all the choice. As a matter of fact, this world is the way it is because you exercise choice and create it this way (whether you know it or not).
The way this world is—is.	The way you create this world determines the possibilities that you have.
This world does not pre-dispose you to any action.	This world not only pre-disposes you, it often propels you into action.
This world has no impact on your results.	This world has a great impact on your results. Because it is this world that pre-disposes you into action, and actions give you results.

Source: © Sameer Dua, Founder, the Institute for Generative Leadership, India

in the present (your actions may or may not be transparent to you) are leading you to a future. This is the default future. And this default future may be transparent to you.

The observer you are may not be consciously 'seeing' this default future.

I had a meeting with the vice-president of Learning and Development at a multinational auto company. Their sales in India had dipped by 5 per cent and 7 per cent, respectively, over the last 2 years. Her claim was that the sales team had reasons for the dip in sales. However, her concern was that they were all satisfied with these reasons and were doing nothing to change things. She stated that this year they were headed towards a further decrease in sales of about 7–8 per cent. She then hastily added, 'but the good news is that our parent company continues to support us, and because we are doing well in certain other countries, we are not taking a big financial hit'.

I asked her, 'would your parent company continue to support you if you had losses of 7–8 per cent every year after 3 years?'

She had a look of question on her face, knowing that eventually, if not after 3 years—maybe 5 years, the parent company will say 'enough is enough'. We cannot support a loss-making region. However, she wanted to believe that they would. The look on her face showed the internal conflict in her head.

This eventual default future was transparent to her. In this short conversation, the default future got revealed to her. We will discuss 'default future' later in Chapter 7 dedicated to it. The point here is that your default future may be transparent to you—only because of the observer you are. You can choose to be the observer who lifts the veil of transparency[8] from the default future.

Once the veil of transparency is lifted, you have new awareness.

And when you have a new awareness, you have a new choice—a choice for a new action. This choice was not available to you while the default future was transparent to you.

Just for purposes of understanding, when I use the word 'future', what I am referring to is everything after this particular moment. A CEO of a company once mentioned to me, 'Every time you say future, I presume a future that is distant from where we are today—maybe 2–3 years ahead. I did not realize when you say future, it includes even 5 minutes from now'.

For example, if a driver drinks alcohol in good measure and drives a car at 120 kph, there is a default future of him having an accident. And that default future is not 2, 3 or 5 years ahead. It could be only a few minutes in the future. Similarly, if I have coffee just before sleeping, I have to be aware of my default future that I will not get sleep soon that night. The caffeine intake will change the chemistry of my brain and block the action of a natural brain chemical that is associated with sleep.

Not too long ago, I coached a senior vice-president (financial products) in a global IT company. After 6 months, he was requested to move to the USA and take responsibility for a larger geography. Another person from Bengaluru moved to Pune and took on this role of my coachee. I was brought on as a coach for this new person too.

It was very interesting for me to see that both of them worked in the same organization, both had exactly the same role, more or less the same team, the same boss, the same market they operated in and the same clients. Everything in the 'outside world' was the same.

However, the way they saw the world was completely different. Each saw different challenges, each saw different opportunities and each saw different areas of improvement for the team.

Based on what each saw, each took different actions. And because each took different actions, they had different results. I am not commenting whether or not these results were better than the other. They certainly were completely different results.

Summary and Reconstruction of Our Understanding

1. A process is transparent when we are unaware of the functioning, or the presence of that process. Depending on the observer we are, our attention is always on something or the other, and at that moment, everything else is transparent to us, that is, we are not aware of the functioning or the presence of that process.

2. What we 'see' is a function of what we go 'looking' for. At a very subconscious level, if you go looking for the impossibility of a task, what you find is evidence for the impossibility of that task. Similarly, if you go looking for the possibility of that task, what you find is evidence for the possibility of that task. And hence, as a leader, the following two fundamental questions are:

   • What are you looking for?
   • Does what you are looking for work for you?

3. The common-sense understanding of our culture is that the world you see is a function of what is 'out there'. However, the claim of this book is, 'the world you see is a function of the observer you are'. You live in two worlds, one is the physical world, and the other is the linguistic world that you create and manifest. The physical world is the same for everyone. However, it is this linguistic world that you create, which determines

   • how you show up in the world,
   • what actions you take and
   • what results you have.

4. As a leader, when you choose to be an observer who observes yourself to be at the source of every relationship, and for that matter, every result that you currently have, you in effect give yourself the power to transform every relationship and every result.
   This is a context shifting way of looking at life, and is very powerful. When people blame others, they literally give away power to cause a shift.

5. The way the world occurs to a CEO of an organization is different from the way the world occurs to a front-line employee of the same organization. The physical world 'out there' is the same. It is the linguistic world of interpretations and assessments of the two that differs. This world is built through a different history of learning, experiences and practices.

6. Your default future is your probable, almost certain future and is based on your assumptions that may be transparent to you. It is not in your conscious awareness that your actions or your inactions in the present (your actions may or may not be transparent to you) are leading you to a future. This is the default future. And this default future may be transparent to you.

7. The objective of this chapter was for you to see that there are many things going on in your world that are transparent to you. When there is an interruption in that transparency, an opportunity to declare a breakdown presents itself. In the following chapter, we will discuss interruptions that require coping.

Generative Practices

1. This chapter made a claim that 'you get what you look for', and also shared an exercise of 'looking for the green'. Based on that, in your journal, make a note of 'what green did you find today? Is that the green you went looking for?'

2. Further to the earlier point, also journal, while 'looking for the green', what did you miss seeing?

3. What does the claim 'the world you see is function of the observer you are' mean to you? Become aware of what is transparent to you in this moment.

4. Get present to the linguistic world that you are creating and that you have created.

5. Think of everything that you do in your day and become present and aware of the actions you take that are transparent to you.

6. Look around you and get present to different people and the contributions they make to your life that are currently transparent to you.

7. Make a daily entry in your journal of the earlier practices as part of 'tuning up your observing' and seeing new possibilities for yourself.

Notes

1. http://www.oxforddictionaries.com/definition/english/transparent, accessed 16 February 2016.
3. Charles Duhigg, *The Power of Habit* (New York: Random House, 2012).
2. Peter J. Denning and Robert Dunham in their book *The Innovator's Way* referred to this from the following book: Bruce H. Lipton, *The Biology of Belief* (Santa Rosa, CA: Mountain of Love/Elite Books, 2005).
4. Peter J. Denning and Robert Dunham, *The Innovator's Way: Essential Practices for Successful Innovation* (Cambridge, MA: MIT Press, 2010).
5. http://www.thehealthsite.com/diseases-conditions/top-8-interesting-facts-about-the-human-eye/, accessed 16 February 2016.
6. I attended The Art and Practice of Ontological Coaching programme of Newfield Network, USA, and that is where I first heard this claim. I found this very powerful, and this has stayed with me ever since. As a part of the programme, we were given a book called *Language and the Pursuit of Happiness* by Chalmers Brothers. This claim is also made in this book.
7. Steve Zaffron and Dave Logan, *The Three Laws of Performance: Rewriting the Future of Your Organization and Your Life* (San Francisco: Jossey-Bass/Wiley/Times Group Books, 2009).
8. Veil of transparency: The veil of transparency is the cover that conceals transparency. To lift the veil of transparency would mean to disclose or uncover transparency—it is to make what was earlier transparent to you, obvious.

4

Interruptions That Require Coping

Our life is full of interruptions. These interruptions could be of any kind, personal or professional, in the area of health, finance, relationships or any other area that matters to an individual, an organization, a family, a group of people or a nation. When there is a break in the transparent flow of action in a way that we need to attend to this interruption, we call it an interruption that requires coping. We have choices to make, possible actions to take.

What was once invisible to us is made obvious and brought to our present awareness by interruptions. Interruptions bring the attention and our awareness to the actions that we are performing and to the events happening around us and concerning us—those actions or events that were invisible to us before the interruption took place.

They make our world appear with all its intricacies and all its complexities. For example, once the space bar on the keyboard stops functioning, it makes the computer suddenly appear as an intricate and a complex machine.

These interruptions also interrupt our future actions. For example, when a businessman is flying from New York to San Francisco, the transparent future of that person is that he will get to San Francisco and attend the client meeting. If he misses his flight to San Francisco, the future that he was expecting has changed and there is an interruption in his transparent future. Some observers assess interruptions to be problems or as negative events.

Our claim is that interruptions are nothing but a break in your transparency. The interruption disrupts an 'established order', and this established order was transparent till the 'interruption' took place.

I have had asthma since I was 7 years old. Every time I get an asthma attack, it interrupts the transparency of my breathing. It brings my focused attention back to breathing, which was transparent to me until I had the asthma attack.

Another example here can be of typing on the computer keyboard, which is habitual and automatic, that is, transparent action, where we do not even see what we are doing; it is just happening through habit. If while typing, the space bar stops functioning, it then causes an interruption in the flow of typing. This has to be coped with in some way because the person typing observes that the proposal document needs to be sent out to the client before the end of the day.

If something happens that leads us to a different assessment of what it is we can expect in the future, we would call this an interruption. An interruption *implies a change in our space of possibilities*. What we assumed was possible before may no longer be possible or what we assumed may not be possible before may suddenly become a possibility. Whenever the observer assesses the space of possibility has changed, be it in a positive or a negative way, that observer is facing an interruption.[1]

The interruption is also an interruption of movement to the default future, both near term and long term. It may delay our moving to the default future, or even change that future. It also opens the possibility of designing and creating that new future.

The interruption can interrupt

- our attention,
- our behaviour,
- our practice,
- our expectations of the present and/or
- our interpretation of the future we are moving towards.

An employee calling in sick at work can be viewed as an interruption that may need to be coped with, or not, depending upon the observer's view of the importance of the role of this employee who has called in sick. This interruption can interrupt any or all of the above-listed parameters, that is, our attention, our behaviour for the day, our practice, our expectations of the present and our expectations of the future we are moving towards.

There could be several causes of these interruptions, including accidents, pleasant surprises, events in the world or our assessments that arise. Our coping response may vary from paralysis and no action to declaring a breakdown and proactively dealing with it.

However, it is interesting to point out here, very often in English, we refer to new opportunities as breaks. For example, when a person receives a new job, or a promotion, or a new client—we often say 'He got a great break!' The reason we call an opportunity a break is because it breaks the transparency of our present. And a break is the same thing as an interruption.

People generally use words such as 'positive' or 'negative'; however, 'positive' or 'negative' is only our interpretation, and these assessments of positive or negative are not a constitutive element of the interruption itself.

The Role of the Observer

As has been discussed earlier, an interruption occurs when the space of possibilities has changed. Something that was assumed to take place or to be possible did not take place or is not possible any more. Similarly, something that was assumed not to take place or not to be possible suddenly takes place or becomes possible.

Each of these assumptions that have been referred earlier is made, most times, at a very subconscious level, by a particular individual, group of individuals, organizations or even nations.

The point here is that these assumptions are not 'out there' in the world. An observer is making these assumptions, that is, a person or a group of persons seeing in a particular way. An event becomes an interruption when the observer in question assesses that the event modifies what was otherwise expected. Each observer will deal with the situation as per their assessment. In the same situation, two different observers may have two different assessments and that will lead to two different actions.

Transparency exists in the observer. What may be transparent to one may not be transparent to another. And since the transparency exists in the observer, the interruption also exists in the observer. The observer takes a view that what has happened or is happening is different from what was expected to happen.

A coachee who earlier worked as a director at a call centre narrated in passing to me her observation about a situation at her work. She said, 'once in a while, when there is a downtime (total shutdown of systems due to a glitch in the server), the mixed reactions of employees are worth a watch'.

'Some tele-callers take a deep sigh and mutter out a "Thank God". They then look at the nearest person to see their reaction and if the reaction is the same, they start off a gossip session. Meanwhile, some team leaders are different observers, they immediately call for a team meeting to utilize the time effectively.'

She used this simple scenario to explain her understanding of interruptions and how this may be assessed as a positive interruption by some and assessed as a negative interruption by others, depending on the observers they were. Based on the observers they were, each took different actions.

The reason we use the word 'observer' here is also because the way you see in one moment can be different from the way you see in another moment.

What Is Disclosive Space?

An interruption is associated with the context you live in and the context is associated with what is called the disclosive space. According to Charles Spinosa, Fernando Flores and Hubert Dreyfus, disclosive space is an 'organized set of practices for dealing with oneself, other people, and things that produces a relatively self contained web of meanings'.[2]

Your disclosive space is the way the world occurs to you. It is not the way the world is; it is the way it occurs to you.

Your disclosive space is your common sense, that is, the totality of your interpretations, your assessments and your habits that disclose a world to you. This space exists in the realm of *you don't even know that you don't know.*

Your disclosive space is your *already always orientation* towards the world. It is already there and it is invisible to you; and, yet it impacts the way the world shows up for you.

It is interesting that Spinosa, Flores and Dreyfus used the word 'space', because it is through this space, or through this vantage point, that a particular world gets disclosed to you.

The key elements of the disclosive space that shape your future are:

- Your cares and concerns
- Your standards and practices of action and coping
- Your moods and emotions
- The possibilities that you see
- Your purposes and 'the games you play'
- Your style

Each of the above-mentioned elements determines what world gets revealed or disclosed to you. This is the key point—the understanding of this term is important because it states how *we shape what* we *see in this world.* It is the opening that each one of us provides for the world to emerge in the way it does for each one of us. As we go deeper, you will see how each of these elements determines how we see the world (Figure 4.1).

Let us look at how some of these elements impact your disclosive space.

Care and Concerns

Personally, I have a care for the state of organ donation in India. Hundreds of thousands of people are dying for the want of organs, and simultaneously, organs are being buried and burnt—those very organs that could save lives. Considering that this is my care, the way the world shows up for me when I read newspapers, or visit hospitals, or even when I surf the Internet or my social media

Figure 4.1   The Key Elements of the Space That Get Disclosed for You

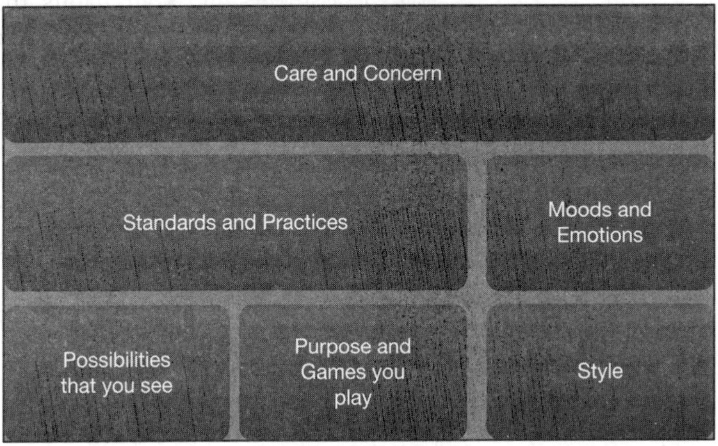

pages is different from the world that shows up for people who do not have this care.

Similarly, a dear friend of mine, Dilip Kukreja, has a care for juvenile diabetes. The way the world shows up for him is different than the way it shows up for me. For example, when he reads a newspaper, he 'sees' news items on diabetes and juvenile diabetes, while I completely miss seeing these news items in the same newspaper. Similarly, I always notice articles on organ donation, and he misses seeing articles on organ donation.

We are reading the same newspaper, but our disclosive space, in the area of our care and concern, is different, and hence while we look at the same newspaper, our eyes pick up different articles, and miss the others.

When I talk about cares, I am not only talking about care for social causes. In the case of a lady I knew, her care was to retain her job, because she felt threatened by the competitive environment in her organization. Because this was her care, the world showed up differently for her. She did not miss an opportunity to gift, send a card or compliment a senior colleague so that she could get into their good books. This is how the world showed up for her inside of her disclosive space based on her care and concerns.

Your Standards and Practices

People have different standards for different things. I met an author recently, and in our first meeting, I got to the café where we were to meet 10 minutes before our scheduled time. She was already there before me. I stated to her that I was hoping I would reach the café before her so that she did not have to wait for me. Her response was, 'You will never find me late for any meeting. I believe people who are not on time are not professional and I would never want to work with such people'.

While I am not going to get into the merit of what she stated, what is important to see is that if I had reached that meeting late, based on her standard and her practice of arriving early, I would have shown up in her world as unprofessional.

These practices determine not only how we show up in the world but also how we perceive the world.

Your Moods and Emotions

Imagine a hypothetical situation:

Robert and his wife had an argument early in the morning. Their daughter is upset with Robert because the previous evening he did not allow the daughter to watch her favourite movie and insisted that she sleep at her scheduled bedtime. The energy in their house is intense with no one talking to each other, and everyone is angry with someone or the other.

In this emotion, Robert leaves to drop his daughter to school. He forgets to put on music in the car and continues to think of the argument with his wife and how unreasonable she has been with him. He drops his daughter to school and starts to head to work. While driving, a motorbike comes and hits his car from behind.

Robert gets really angry and gets out of his car, yelling at the biker. He gives him a piece of his mind and verbally abuses him.

Now, let us change the situation at their home:

Robert and his wife had a lovely morning together. They had tea together, spoke about each of their plans for the day and even scheduled their weekend plan to take a short vacation over Saturday and Sunday. Their daughter slept on time after watching her favourite movie and woke up on time for school in a great mood. Robert and his daughter leave home happy.

As soon as Robert sits in the car, he puts on music and his daughter and he sing along. Robert drops his daughter to school and then continues to head to work, listening to his favourite music. While driving, a motorbike comes and hits his car from behind.

Robert does not get angry; he looks at the young man driving his motorbike and gets reminded of his times on the motorbike. He tells the biker to be careful and starts to head back to work.

In both the cases, the event that took place was exactly the same: *while driving, a motorbike comes and hits Robert's car from behind.*

However, the mood or emotion he was in when this event took place determined how the world showed up for him. *The event did not change; the way the world showed up for him changed.* Robert's disclosive space changed.

Possibilities that You See

If you are out looking for certain possibilities, the world that will get disclosed to you will be a world with these possibilities. Very recently, I was in a coaching conversation with my coachee who just could not see any possibilities in his relationship with his subordinate. The way the world continued to get disclosed to him with regard to his subordinate was a world where his subordinate was unreasonable and not understanding of the problems of my coachee. When I invited him to see possibilities in this relationship, a lot opened up for my coachee, and a *new* subordinate emerged for him. Different aspects of the subordinate's personality were revealed (or disclosed) to my coachee, which were not revealed earlier to him.

My brother-in-law Parag is a keen observer of possibilities. He is perpetually 'looking for' new possibilities. And guess what shows up for him over and over again! New possibilities. A senior colleague that I worked with continued to look for 'problems' in every opportunity. And guess how the world disclosed itself to this colleague! He continued to only see new insurmountable problems.

Your Purpose and 'The Games You Play'

What game are you playing? Are you playing a game of your personal growth? Are you playing a game of pulling a colleague down? Are you playing a game for the team's growth and success? Or are you playing the game of the organization's growth?

What we mean by 'games' is not something for entertainment. We have very serious games in life, the game of career, of marriage, of living our lives. Most of the games we are involved in were not consciously chosen by us, and we may not even be aware of them.

Depending on your purpose and the games that you play—a world gets disclosed to you. If you are playing the game of personal growth—you will 'see' opportunities for personal growth. If you are playing a game of pulling a colleague down—you will 'see' opportunities to do so. Or rather, these opportunities will 'show up' or get disclosed to you, because that is the game you are playing—consciously or subconsciously.

Your Style

Your style has a lot to do with your practices. For instance, in one of the local chamber of commerce meetings, a CEO of a significantly large real estate company mentioned to me on arriving late: 'I never arrive on time. It makes me seem desperate, and I do not want to give the impression that I am desperate to the world'.

The way the world gets disclosed to this CEO as compared to the author to whom I referred earlier in this section is completely different.

If you really get the claim made in the previous chapter, *the world you see is a function of the observer you are*, you will start to see your disclosive space has a lot to do with what world gets disclosed to you. As a matter of fact, *you only see the world that gets disclosed to you, given the observer you are*.

If you get aware of your disclosive space, you have a choice to recreate your disclosive space, and open up possibilities, those that were not available to you earlier, for a new world to show up for you.

Interruptions That Impact Possibilities

Some interruptions open possibilities and can be assessed as positive interruptions. Then there are interruptions that close possibilities and can be assessed as negative interruptions. The birth of a baby, for instance, is a happy event in the life of most parents. It brings about tremendous changes in their lives. Until then the parents were used to a particular routine like unwinding over a cup of tea together every evening or going out to movies once a week, and they were even used to all the things in the house being organized in a particular way and knew exactly where everything was kept.

With the arrival of a child, there is an interruption in the routine of their daily lives. That a particular routine existed was transparent to the parents. They now have a child to take care of. They may no longer get time to spend with each other alone; they are no longer aware of where things are kept because they now focus their attention on their child and do not find it important to keep things back in the place they were meant to be. It brings them joy to put everything on hold and concentrate their attention on their child.

The arrival of a child interrupts the transparency of the present, and that of the future, for the parents. It may open up new possibilities in certain areas, and close possibilities in certain areas. For example, with the arrival of my first daughter, given the observer my wife was, she took a break from her teaching career, and hence this interruption of having a child closed possibilities in the domain of her career. And yet, she was extremely excited because it opened a whole new domain of possibilities for her and for us as parents. It changed our default future.

Similarly, getting a new job or a new assignment within an existing job, or getting a new contract, can all be assessed as interruptions. While these may certainly be interruptions in your existing transparency, they may positively impact your life.

Physical sickness can be assessed as a negative interruption, one that closes possibilities. The concerned person's daily routine gets disrupted and his body goes through discomfort and pain, which is an interruption in his normal healthy way of living. However, as a child when I went to school, I assessed physical sickness then as a positive interruption because it meant I could miss school (while I did not understand the concept of interruptions, I was happy I was unwell then).

Ranjit Nair worked as a senior human resource manager for a chain of 5-star hotels. He was awarded a promotion and the designation of an assistant vice-president. For Ranjit Nair, this was an interruption that opened new possibilities for him When you are awarded a promotion at work, it is generally assessed as an interruption that opens up new possibilities for your work life. Your accountabilities increase, and you have new reportees and a new future to achieve. Ranjit Nair was no different.

However, along with other perks also came a change of workplace. Ranjit would now be required to travel about 4 hours to and from work every day. Ranjit was happy initially, but soon he started detesting the daily travel and began to lose interest in his work. What started out for him as a jump in his career now started becoming a reason for his daily discomfort. In a few months, Ranjit started looking for another job. This same interruption that earlier opened up possibilities for Ranjit now closed possibilities for him He was now a different observer than when he was initially offered the promotion.

Earlier, the promotion occurred to him as an interruption that opened new possibilities (in his career). Later, this same interruption of the promotion seemed like one that closed possibilities (for his health and family time).

Nothing changed in the world 'out there'. All that changed was the way Ranjit Nair observed.

A divorce can also be assessed as a negative interruption by some observers and a positive interruption by some other observers.

Cultures assess certain interruptions to be positive or negative. For example, for certain cultures in India, if a 25-year-old man gets married and leaves his parents' home, it may be considered as a negative interruption for the parents. The same may not be considered as a negative interruption within certain other cultures in India, or even in the Western culture.

The point I am making here is as follows:

1. Interruptions exist in the observer that you are.
2. For some observers, an event may be an interruption, and for some others, it may not be an interruption because they were expecting that event to take place.
3. Depending on the observer you are, an interruption may open up possibilities for you, or may close possibilities for you and based on that you may label it as 'positive' or 'negative'.
4. How you determine whether an interruption opens up possibilities or closes possibilities has to do with your cultural and historical background, your care, your commitments and your standards for taking care of your concerns at the time in your life.

Why 'Interruptions' and Not 'Problems'?

I cannot emphasize enough that the observer you are, or the way you look at events or the internal conversations you have with yourself when an event takes place, will prompt your future actions, which in turn has an impact on your results.

One of the reasons I have used the concept of interruptions in this book, rather than problems or opportunities, is because the common-sense understanding of our culture is that problems and opportunities exist by and of themselves. Problems are also known as troubles, hindrances or snags and have a negative impact on the internal conversations that are created. Interruptions do not exist by and of themselves, and they are what they are only because of the observer we are.

Let us distinguish the two words 'interruptions' and 'problems' and notice a sea of difference in the way the issue occurs to us when we call it a problem or when we call it an interruption.

1. When something is intended and that does not happen, and for you that is not how it should be, then it is a problem. An interruption is when a transparent flow of action is

interrupted in a way that you must attend to it, and consider what actions you must take in response.

2. Problems are always assessed as negative. Interruptions could be assessed as negative or as positive, depending on the observer. Irrespective of whether this is assessed as negative or positive, the posture of responding to a problem is different from the posture of responding to an interruption.

3. Problems are assessed to be 'out there' (it is generally stated 'I have a problem' as if there is something distinguishable from you that you have). *The concept of interruptions allows us to observe that difficulties and opportunities are what they are because of the way we 'see' the situation. They do not exist independent of the observer.*

This is not just an issue of semantics (*and assuming it was an issue of semantics, even then, we need to respect semantics. Semantics determine how we see our world*). It is how the world shows up for you when you observe something to be as an interruption as compared to how the world shows up for you when you observe something to be a problem.

In interruptions, you choose an assessment you want to make, rather than going blindly with an automatic assessment. You choose an assessment, because it is assessments that yield actions and actions that yield results. And at the end of the day, it is all about results. (We will discuss the distinction of assessment in detail in Chapter 6.)

Sources of the Interruption

There can be different sources of interruption. Figure 4.2 shows a quadrant that explains the sources of interruptions.

External Sources

External sources of interruptions are where you have no control in the causation of the interruption, that is, you are not at the source of creating the interruptions. These are caused with no active participation of yours.

Figure 4.2 Sources of Interruption

External Unintentional	External Intentional
Internal Unintentional	Internal Intentional

1. The first external source of interruption is natural events (these are not intended by someone else) that take place and cause an interruption in your transparency. Examples include a death in the family, a tsunami, a hurricane and so on. I call these External-Unintentional sources of interruptions.

2. The other type of an external interruption is when actions of other people cause an interruption in transparency for you. For example, a member of your team leaves the organization, the tenant does not pay you your rental dues on time, you receive an unexpected inheritance and so on. I call these external events caused by human beings that cause interruptions as External-Intentional sources of interruptions.

Internal Sources

Internal sources of interruptions are when you are at the source of creating the interruptions.

3. You can be at the source of the interruption without wanting to actively cause the interruption. For example, rash driving may lead to an accident. While you did not want to cause the interruption, *your* fast driving caused the interruption. You were at the source of the interruption, yet it was an accident and you did not want to cause this accident. I call these Internal-Unintentional sources of interruptions.

4. Perhaps the most important interruptions are the ones that are caused because you declare a breakdown as a conscious act of design. When you are dissatisfied with something

and you choose to change the order of things, you have a choice to declare a breakdown, and when you do so, you create an interruption in transparency. These are Intentional-Interruptions caused by you. This is when you are being generative and causing a future of your choice, maybe for yourself, your family, your team, your organization , your nation, or the world—rather than being resigned to a default future.

In all my work of consulting, coaching and training, and interacting with people across hierarchies and across nationalities, I have come to a conclusion: *that every person who is even remotely successful by their own standard is successful because at some point in time, he or she chose to declare a breakdown—they decided that their default future was not acceptable to them, and created a new future, and thereby causing interruptions to their transparent flow of life.* These people end up doing or achieving something that was not considered ordinary by others.

Declaring Breakdowns as an Important Leadership Move

What do you do with your life? Do you *walk* your life? Do you *run* your life? Do you *jog* your life?

What is it that you do with your life?

You *lead* your life. That is right. That is what is always said. You 'lead' your life!

My claim is that all of us are leaders. However, many of us do not exercise our full-blown leadership in our own lives, perhaps because we do not 'see' ourselves as in control of our lives.

So, how do you exercise your leadership? To understand that, let us understand who is a leader.

A leader is someone who

- *creates* an extraordinary future,
- gets others to *commit* to this new extraordinary future and
- *generates and coordinates action* with others to achieve this new future.[3]

What Does Creating an Extraordinary Future Mean?

For the purpose of this book, an extraordinary future means a future that is different from the default future. It is a future that is beyond the usual. When you create an extraordinary future, it means you as a leader have chosen to declare a breakdown. You state that if the normal course of events were to take place, and if you did not actively participate in changing this course, you would end up in a particular future. This future is not okay for you. You want to choose to be at another destination, and that destination is extraordinary, given the current perceived circumstances.

So, the claim of this book is: *to exercise your full-blown leadership, you have to be skilled in declaring breakdowns in your life.*

I met Roger Weatherman in one of my consulting assignments in the UK. He was the production head of a mid-sized manufacturing company there. In this organization, most of the work was done using old technology. The workers came to work every day and went about their daily activities, manufacturing the products upto 90-95 per cent of the capacity of the unit. The shareholders were satisfied, the management team was satisfied and the workers were also content. However, it was transparent to them that they could increase their capacity by 70 per cent, by introducing new technology.

Business was growing, demand for their products had increased in the recent past, and yet supply was capped based of the capacity of the manufacturing unit.

However, Roger Weatherman was not satisfied. He wanted to take advantage of the growing demand for their products. He chose to declare a breakdown. He recommended to the management team to induct new technology at a capital expenditure of £2 million. He showed the financial numbers to the management team and how this new technology would increase their capacity by 70 per cent and double their profitability.

Roger Weatherman's act of declaring a breakdown created an interruption for the entire organization. The transparency of the present and the future was interrupted for the management and the employees of the organization. Roger introduced the new technology and enabled the workers to operate it. The workers upgraded their skills, and as a result, their time and efforts are now used far more productively.

(Continued)

(*Continued*)

Roger Weatherman intentionally declared a breakdown in the otherwise transparent procedures to reduce the waste of time, money and effort. His organization's probable yet almost certain future of no significant improvement in the production numbers and profitability was not acceptable to him.

Bringing in new technology meant

- seeking funding from lending institutions,
- rewriting all process notes,
- training employees in the use of this new technology and
- overcoming several other operational challenges.

In the interest of increasing their capacity and doubling their profitability, the organization went ahead with this new technology and greatly benefitted from it, financially, and also in providing greater work satisfaction for their employees.

The greater your ability to see new possibilities and question the status quo, the more successful you can be. Questioning status quo means to intentionally create interruptions, to achieve a future of choice rather than one dictated by drift.

IGL, India, the organization that I founded in partnership with IGL, USA, received a requirement from an organization that is a part of a $70 billion German group. This organization wanted to change their culture and have a new high-performance culture.

What this organization was doing was declaring a breakdown, and causing an interruption. They acknowledged that the culture they had did not work for them any more. This was despite the fact that in certain areas, this organization was judged to be world-class.

People regularly create breakdowns, thereby creating interruptions—it is just that we do not know that we are doing so. This book is an endeavour to bring this into our conscious realm so that we can continue to do so, not out of default, but out of choice. And do it effectively.

Disharmonies Create Opportunities

When an interruption takes place, and you need to cope with it, our claim is one way you can cope with an interruption is by declaring a breakdown (Chapter 5 is on declaring breakdowns).

When you sense a certain disharmony, you have a choice to declare a breakdown. In this case, when you declare the breakdown, without an interruption, the breakdown causes an interruption that needs to be coped with for the people concerned. This is a powerful leadership move, and a powerful move in shifting your life's drift (Figure 4.3).

Sensing disharmony[4] means

• you feel something is not right;
• you feel something is missing;
• something in your gut says this is not headed where you want it to go; or
• you feel the anxiety to do more, to achieve more.

This sensing[5] is just a place to start. Once you have articulated, what is it that is not working for you, you have a choice to declare a breakdown. Creating breakdowns is a skill that gets developed as you practise. It is a practice where you start to listen for disharmonies in the environment, and see how you can declare a breakdown to the transparent flow to establish a new order, a new flow—one that works for you, your team or your organization. These disharmonies are a place to look for to declare a breakdown.

Sometimes you need to stay with these disharmonies and allow them to grow so that clarity may emerge. People very easily ignore these disharmonies, and lose out on opportunities for creating new futures for themselves and their organizations.

My daughter, when she was 8 years old, out of nowhere came and told me, 'dad, you know, I have just discovered that I am

Figure 4.3 Interruptions and Declarations

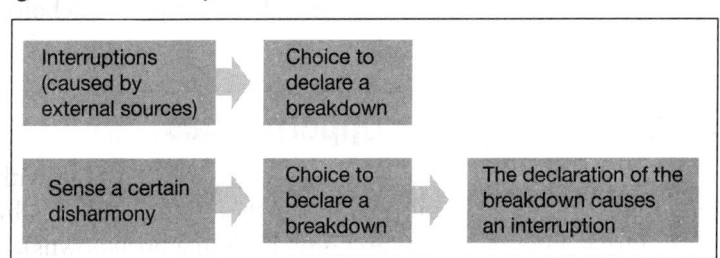

shy!' Let me create some context here. My daughter has been an above-average student in academics, actively participating is extra-curricular activities, and sports activities. Suddenly, she claimed in her conversation that she 'discovered' that she was shy. As if that she was shy was hidden from her up until that moment! It was blind to her that she did not discover that she was 'shy'; she created she was shy in her declaration (we will discuss the speech and listening act of declaration in Chapter 5).

I felt a cringe in my body when she stated this. I thought, 'this "I am shy" conversation my daughter has had with herself may now become the context for her future participation in her school and extra-curricular activities'. A few days later, I noticed it indeed had started to show up for her as real. She started to behave in coherence with this creation of hers. When my friends came over, those who she was very fond of, she started to hide and would not want to meet them. She would tell me, 'dad, you know I am shy, right?'

I started sensing this disharmony in my body. A few questions came in to my mind:

- I was taught four languages in school. How come no one taught or showed me the creative power of language?
- How come no one taught me that you do not discover *you are shy*, but you create *you are shy*?

I stayed with these disharmonies for over a year, allowing these to grow in me. From this disharmony, I declared a breakdown. A new company, CREO Learning LLP, came into existence, which my brother, Prashant Dua, and I set up in partnership. I decided that because I was not taught the creative power of language did not mean that my daughter's generation, and generations after that, will also not be taught this. In partnership with Red Tree Design Studio, we created new storybook characters called Milk and Honey, and using *the world of Milk and Honey*, we intend to enter schools and teach students the immense power of language.

The point that I am making here is that when you sense a disharmony, you are actually being presented with an opportunity to unveil a blindness that you have lived with. It was blind to us that we could be at the source of taking generative leadership education to schools, teaching students the power of language, or the phenomenon of language.

Thus, in conclusion of this chapter, the claim that I am making is that there are either of two things that happen before you can declare a breakdown:

- There is an interruption that needs to be coped with, or
- You sense a disharmony in some area of your care.

Part II of this book deals with the process of declaring and dealing with a breakdown.

Summary and Reconstruction of Our Understanding

1. Our life is full of interruptions, and some that require to be coped with. When there is a break in the transparent flow of action in a way that we need to attend to this interruption, we call it an interruption that requires coping.
2. Our claim is that interruptions are nothing but a break in your transparency. An interruption disrupts the 'established order', and this established order was transparent till the 'interruption' took place.
3. An interruption implies a change in our space of possibilities. What we assumed was possible before may no longer be possible or what we assumed may not be possible before may suddenly become a possibility.
4. An interruption may interrupt our attention, our behaviour, our practice, our expectations and our interpretation of the future we are moving towards. It affects our assessment of our default future.
5. What was once invisible to us is made obvious and brought to our present awareness by interruptions. Interruptions bring the attention and our awareness to the actions that we are performing and to the events happening around us and concerning us—those actions or events that were invisible to us before the interruption took place.

6. Often in English, we refer to new opportunities as breaks. These breaks are nothing but interruptions.

7. Transparency exists in the observer. What may be transparent to one may not be transparent to another. And since the transparency exists in the observer, the interruption also exists in the observer. The observer takes a view that what has happened or is happening is different from what was expected to happen.

8. Your disclosive space is your common sense, that is, the totality of your interpretations, your assessments and your habits that disclose a world to you. This space exists in the realm of *you don't even know that you don't know*.

9. Your disclosive space is your *already always orientation* towards the world. It is already there and it is invisible to you; and, yet it impacts the way the world shows up for you.

10. Your disclosive space is the way the world occurs to you. It is not the way the world is; it is the way it occurs to you.

11. Some interruptions open possibilities and can be assessed as positive interruptions. Then there are interruptions that close possibilities and can be assessed as negative interruptions. The observer determines whether an interruption closes or opens possibilities.

12. An important claim of this book: to exercise your full-blown leadership, you have to be skilled in declaring breakdowns in your life.

13. The greater your ability to see new possibilities and question the status quo, the more successful you can be. Questioning status quo means to intentionally declare breakdowns, to achieve a future of choice rather than one dictated by fate.

14. The distinction between problem and interruption is not just an issue of semantics. It is how the world shows up for you when you observe something to be as an interruption as compared to something being a problem. In interruptions, you choose an assessment you want to make, rather than going blindly with an automatic assessment.

15. Declaring breakdowns is a skill that gets developed as you practise. It is a practice where you start to listen for disharmonies in the environment, and see how you can

create an interruption to the transparent flow to establish a new order, a new flow—one that works for you, your team or your organization. This is a powerful leadership move, and a powerful move in life to take care of what you care about.

Generative Practices

1. Explore how the interruptions that you chose to create helped you to be where you are today in your life.
2. Think of a time in your recent past, when an external interruption took place in your life. If that same interruption were to happen to you now, how would you observe that interruption?
3. Make a daily entry in your journal of the above practices for the sake of widening and deepening your capacity to observe and create possibilities for what you care about.
4. Please continue to engage in the practices of the earlier chapters. Let practices at the end of each chapter not replace practices recommended in the previous chapters, but have new practices build on previous ones.

Notes

1. This has been adapted from Rafael Echeverria's (of Newfield Network) paper on 'Moods and Emotions'. While he calls this a break in transparency, I have called this an interruption, as we do at IGL. At Newfield Network, there is no distinction between a break in transparency and a breakdown. At IGL, we distinguish a break in transparency as an interruption, and then based on the observer, she/he may declare a breakdown (or not declare a breakdown).
2. C. Spinosa, F. Flores, and H.L. Dreyfus, *Disclosing New Worlds: Entrepreneurship, Democratic Action, and the cultivation of Solidarity* (Cambridge, MA: MIT Press, 1997).
3. Adapted from the works for Werner Erhard and Michael Jensen.
4. The disharmonies term came originally from Spinosa, Dreyfus and Flores' book *Disclosing New Worlds: Entrepreneurship, Democratic Action, and the cultivation of Solidarity.*
5. 'Sensing' as a term has been used by Robert Dunham and Peter Denning in their book *The Innovator's Way.* There is a chapter dedicated to 'sensing' in this book.

PART II

The 6-step Process at a Glance

Here are the 6 steps to designing a future of your choice for yourself, and for your organization. That's what the promise of this book is – to provide you with simple steps to create and achieve a future that works for you. When I say, 'simple', I don't mean 'easy'. These may be simple to understand, but you need to keep practicing these steps to gain mastery of these.

Furthermore, when I say 'simple', I don't mean they are trivial or unimportant. As a matter of fact these are so important that I dare say these are non-discretionary. In some form or other, you need to follow these 6-steps. You can either depend on luck, or follow these steps to achieving your new future of choice.

Once there is an interruption, either created by you, or caused by external circumstances, you have a choice to declare a breakdown.

The 6-step Process to Declaring a Breakdown and Creating a Future of Your Choice

This is a simple 6-step process that has already led many individuals and organizations to breakthrough performances (Figure PII.1). It has helped teams resolve their issues and work with commitment towards what they care about.

Declaring breakdowns is a conversational move for leaders and is an effective way of creating breakthroughs every day. Whether it is a breakdown in your car while going to office or a snag that is encountered or envisioned in the merger of two organizations, this technology is helpful in coping with change and effectively dealing with the situation in hand.

Step 1: Declare a Breakdown

To declare a breakdown is to take a stand. It is a declaration that you will take whatever action is needed to achieve any future that you may create.

Figure PII.1   The 6-step Process to Declaring a Breakdown and Creating a Future of Your Choice

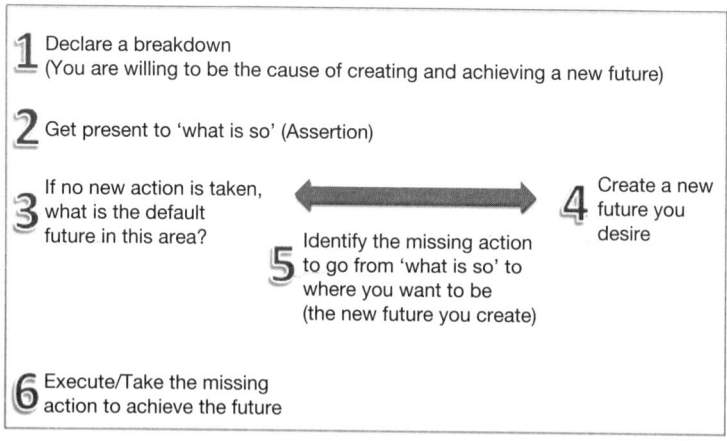

When you declare a breakdown, you declare that you want to exercise choice in matters of your life.

Declaring a breakdown is declaring that you are taking responsibility in a particular matter of your life.

And finally, you declare your own breakdown. Nobody can declare it for you.

Step 2: Get Present to 'What Is So' (Assertion)

The next step is to bring your attention to focus on 'what is so'. You do so by getting present to the assertions in the matter. Assertions are claims of facts that can either be true or false. When you are looking at 'what is so', you look at an action that either happened or did not happen. You look at the situation objectively to establish facts that are observable or measurable or those that can be evidenced.

Most importantly, when you are looking at 'what is so', there are no stories, no justifications, no explanations or no reasons. There are only facts (assertions). What is observable in the world as a fact is not an opinion.

Step 3: If No New Action Is Taken, What Is the Default Future in This Area?

We briefly introduced the default future in the introduction chapter. If no new action is taken, then what is the probable, almost certain future in the matter? Your default future is not evident to you, unless you ask yourself objectively: 'What is my probable, almost certain future in this matter given the current course of action or state of things?'

The answer to this question identifies where you will end up if no new action is taken. Each one of us has a default future in different areas of our life. Most of us are blind to our default future. Some others choose to be observers who want to lift the veil of transparency from their default future. The ones who do so may choose to take action to change this default future.

Step 4: Create a New Future

How do you create a new future? We will deal with this in Step 4 of this process. You create a new future because the default future is not acceptable to you

Step 5: Identify the Missing Action to Go from 'What Is So' Now to 'Where You Want to Be' (the New Future You Create)

Once you have distinguished the default future and have created a new future, the missing actions may become apparent to you. These are the missing actions from 'what is so today' to 'where I want to be'. These missing actions are generative conversational moves/conversational actions.

Step 6: Execution

All of the above is meaningless if you do not execute on your commitments to fill in the gap between 'what is so today' and the 'new future'. At the end of the day, it is only actions that give you results. You must get skilled in order to take actions yourself, and also in calling on your network of help to coordinate actions with others so that the new future/shared future is achieved.

5

Declaring Breakdowns

The Significance of Care

Breakdowns are declared in the areas of care. For example, one morning, I read in the newspaper a leading information technology (IT) company posted a drop in their revenues by 7 per cent. This company is a major IT company in India, and I am interested in news about this company, but it is certainly not a part of my care. I do not work in this company, I have not invested in this company and I do not do any business with this company.

I choose not to declare a breakdown in the matter of this company only because it is not a care of mine.

I have used the word 'care' 203 times in this book. And the reason for giving so much importance to care is because it is central to leadership. You can exercise your leadership only in an area of your care. You can declare meaningful breakdowns only in an area of your care.

Human beings are beings of care. We have different cares, and we are all living to take care of these cares that we have. When we take action to take care of what we care for, we bring meaning in that action. Action that does not take care of any of your cares is a meaningless action.

Results that satisfy us are results in domains of our care. If you have a result, and yet you do not experience satisfaction, then you need to question if that result was in an area of your care.

We can be either connected to our care, or disconnected. In our culture today, we are educated to perform in order to produce external results that others value. We are not trained to go internally to discover our own care. Most clients or participants we work with find the question 'what do you care about' a bit of a surprise. No one has told them that this is an important question and that their answer matters.

It is a crucial question. It reveals the ground of our being as human beings, the foundation for our experience of life.

Since care is fundamental to value and satisfaction, it is also fundamental to business and organizations. It is a blind spot of our culture that care matters fundamentally. We are told that only the external results matter. But that is only if someone cares. Someone needs to care for external results, and that is when they matter.

As part of developing your capacity to take care of what you care about, of course the key question is: *What do you care about?*

One important opportunity in continuing to ask yourself the question of what you care about is that you can begin to distinguish what is it that you truly care about versus what others have said you should care about. You can then re-choose in a way that makes the choice truly yours, rather than it being a 'should'. Is living a certain lifestyle one that you truly choose or one that has been handed down to you unexamined? What about the level of education or attaining certain degrees? Were these things you chose to do or felt you 'should' do because of the expectations of others?

Also by asking the question of 'what we care about', we can begin to see where our actions and cares may be incoherent or incompatible. Do we say we care about our employees, for example, but then every now and then you have a conversation with them that puts them down and invalidates them? Oftentimes, we have something that we care about, but we have never asked ourselves the question: What would it look like to take care of that?

If you panic with the question and your first response is 'I don't know what I care about', do not worry. As human beings, we are creatures of care. A first place to look might be how you spend your time. Work? Family? Community? Health? Environment? Music? Spirituality? Where and how do you spend most of your time? This can begin to show us some of what we care about, including some of what we may only subconsciously care about (such as looking good, staying comfortable and risking or not risking too much).

Care is fundamental to declaring breakdowns. Why would you want to declare a breakdown in a matter that you have no care for? Only when you know what is meaningful, or what is of consequence to you, or what your cares are, that the question arises, 'Am I taking care of what I care about?' And if not, you have a choice to declare a breakdown in that area of your life.

We invite you to get present to what is it that you really care for, and then consider declaring breakdowns in the matter of your care to enable you to take care of what you care about.

Reflective Pause

Take a few moments to reflect on:

What are your different areas of cares?
Once you have identified different domains of cares, the next question for you to reflect upon is:

Are you taking care of your cares?
I invite you to journal your different cares; and then reflect on how well are you taking care of your cares.

Speech and Listening Act: Declaration

In the earlier chapters, we explored what a breakdown is. To be able to effectively declare a breakdown, however, we need to now explore what a 'declaration' is.

Various authors have distinguished the word 'declaration', and I have included a few here:

Declarations are speech acts in which the speaker, out of nothingness, brings forth a new world of possibilities, a new way of seeing things, a new playing field on which to play.

—Chalmers Brothers[1]

The act of bringing something into existence through language; the act of creating the future.

—Bob Dunham[2]

Declaration is owning the future—not just having goals.

—Bob Dunham[3]

A Declaration is an utterance in which some one with authority to do so brings something into being that wasn't there before.

— Mathew Budd and Larry Rothstein[4]

The way I would like to distinguish the word 'declaration' is as follows:

A declaration is a speech and a listening act, made by a person of authority to do so, where he or she, out of nothingness brings forth a new possibility, a new future into existence that they own.

A declaration can begin, resolve or end things.

You will notice that I have taken essential features of all the above definitions and created a new distinction that is all encompassing.

Let us extract the important elements that emerge from this definition, and the earlier definitions.

1. *Declarations are speech and listening acts.* You make a declaration in language and you bring a future into existence through the act of saying it. Organizations declare their vision, judges in courts declare their judgements, sporting

associations declare rules of the game and parents declare deadlines for children to sleep.

All of these are speech acts that bring a future into existence through committed listening. A future gets created in the speaking of someone. Till such a time, it did not exist. It came into existence only through the act of speech and listening.

In a declaration, your word comes before the world, that is, you first create your future in your word and then the world gets created. For example, the preamble of the Constitution of India[5] states:

WE, THE PEOPLE OF INDIA, having solemnly resolved to constitute India into a SOVEREIGN SOCIALIST SECULAR DEMOCRATIC REPUBLIC and to secure to all its citizens:

JUSTICE, social, economic and political;

LIBERTY of thought, expression, belief, faith and worship;

EQUALITY of status and of opportunity; and to promote among them all

FRATERNITY assuring the dignity of the individual and the unity and integrity of the Nation;

IN OUR CONSTITUENT ASSEMBLY this twenty-sixth day of November, 1949, do HEREBY ADOPT, ENACT AND GIVE TO OURSELVES THIS CONSTITUTION.

The Constitution of India was created first (*the word was created first*), and then this Constitution (*the word*) provided the context for future legislations in India. Fundamental Rights of citizens of India were *declared* in the Constitution, and because these have been declared in the Supreme Law of India, I, as a citizen of India, can claim to have these fundamental rights.

2. *Declarations are made out of nothingness.* When a person makes a conscious declaration, one of the important criteria, from my viewpoint, is that she or he comes from a place where there are no past assessments, judgements or conclusions marring that declaration.

For example, while declaring the future of his ₹300 million organization, my coachee declared that he would increase the revenue of his organization by 20 per cent the following year. While many experts will find this to be a perfectly acceptable declaration, I believe it is constrained by the past year's turnover. The coachee had experience in his business, and hence based on his business, he declared a 20 per cent increase.

Experience lies in the past, and to rely on the past to deliver a result in the future may be a mistake. People believe they have 'experience' and that 'experience' tells them what is possible. And that is the core of what I find constraining! You do not need experience to tell you what is possible. You want to make possible what you want to make possible. Then have the gumption and the courage to take on everything to make possible what you want to make possible.

Does that mean that experience is worthless? Not necessarily! Using experience to declare a future may be constraining; however, once you have declared a future, your experience will be of immense use to you in taking actions to achieve that future.

When you use your experience to create a future, you are coming from the past and chances are you are setting an ordinary future. However, if you declare a future of choice first, and then use your experience to achieve that future, there are higher chances of you reaching that future.

In their book *Think Like a Freak*,[6] Steven Levitt and Stephen Dubner give an example of a young man known as Kobi, who had a slight build and was barely 5 feet 8 inches tall. Kobi participated in the Nathan's Famous Fourth of July International Hot Dog Eating Contest, generally held at Coney Island in New York City. The official record stood at a mind-boggling 25 1/8 hot dogs and buns (HDB) in 12 minutes (25 hot dogs plus 1/8 of a hot dog more).

Kobi in his very first contest at Coney Islands set a new world record of 50 HDB in 12 minutes! If you increased by 20 per cent the past world record, it would still only be a little more than 30 HDB in 12 minutes.

This is what I mean by making declarations without getting constrained by the past. Kobi was not restricted by the past record and went on to almost doubling the earlier record.

3. *Declarations bring forth new possibilities (open possibilities or close possibilities), that which did not exist earlier.* When an organization declares its vision, it opens up new possibilities for the organization. When a parent declares a new deadline for bedtime, it closes possibilities for the child. When the International Cricket Council (ICC) declares a new rule of 5 fielders inside the 30-yard circle at all times in an inning, it closes some possibilities and opens certain other possibilities for cricket players.

4. *When you declare, you own the future rather than just having some goals.* A declaration is a context for action, for achieving a future.

   When our fundamental rights were declared in the Constitution of India, it was not a goal to simply achieve. It became the context for all future legislative, executive and judiciary action of this country.

   When the ICC declares a new rule, it is not a goal to follow that rule—this new rule has been brought into existence, and the game will now be played inside of this new rule. Similarly, when you make a declaration, it is not a goal—it is the context of your future action. You own the future, and take actions to make the future happen.

5. *To make a declaration, you need authority to do so.* As a bowler of a cricket team, I cannot declare a new rule that works for me. I do not have the authority.

   In the matter of setting rules for the game of cricket, the authority rests with the ICC.

   In the matter of declaring a vision for the organization, the authority rests with the board of directors.

   In the matter of declaring a person married, the authority rests with the priest.

   In the matter of declaring a divorce, or convicting or declaring someone as guilty, the authority rests with the judge.

   It is important to get that a rule in cricket changes only because the ICC says so, or a marriage happens only because ministers, civil authorities or priests say so. A divorce or a conviction happens only because the judge says so. It is in the declaration of people who have authority to make declarations that the world changes.

Such people have been given the authority by the state or appropriate groups to make these declarations.

Leadership is about having authority in a community to make certain declarations that bring something into existence by the saying of it. The authority may be formal; for example, there are very formal and explicit processes for declaring who is a judge, an umpire or a CEO in a corporation. Less formally, declarations may be granted authority by an audience or a community simply from the force of the speaker's argument, presence and ability to judge the concerns of the listeners. In either case, the essence of declarations is that the speaker of a declaration is authorized by a community to make declarations, and the declarations they make are only effective as long as the community authorizes the speaker and respects the declarations.

When a person is not authorized by a community or granted authority, then a declaration will not be effective and people will not honour it. For example, I am not a judge, and because I am not a judge, I cannot sentence anyone to jail. And if a manager in a company does not have authority granted to them by their subordinates, their orders may not be followed and their declarations not respected.

A key question is, 'Who has authority in the matter of your life?'

In the matter of your life, the authority to make declarations rests with you. You have the authority in the matter of your own life. It is a different thing that we very easily give away this authority to our parents, children, bosses, clients, juniors, friends and, at times, even to random people.

While you certainly have authority in the matter of your life, the next question is, 'Do you give yourself this authority in the matter of your life?'

Authority is the power to influence or command thought, and the root of the word 'authority' comes from the word 'author', which means the 'originator'. So, the above question can be reworded as 'who is authoring *your* life'.

My experience as a leadership coach has been that very few people

1. are aware that they have authority in the matter of their life to make declarations, and,
2. in certain cases, when they are aware, they do not grant themselves this authority.

It is very similar to a manager not being granted authority by his/her subordinates. While the manager seems to have the authority due to his/her position in the organization, his/her subordinates do not grant him/her this authority due to his/her identity or lack of trustworthiness in the organization.

Likewise, many people seem to have authority in the matter of their lives, yet they do not have an identity of themselves or trust themselves enough to grant themselves the authority to make certain declarations.

Reflective Pause

1. Up until now, who has had power in the matter of different areas of your life?
2. Do you give yourself authority in the matter of your life?

Take a moment and reflect on this question.

One last important question: 'Why do you have authority in the matter of your own life?'

And the answer is, 'Because you say so!'

Yes, it is as simple as that. You have authority in the matter of your life, simply because you say so. You can say you do not have authority and you are right—you do not have authority. You can say you have authority and you are right—you have authority in the matter of your life.

Some people give themselves authority in certain areas of their life, and not in certain other areas. This is a function of practice, and you may need to train your body to give yourself authority for your own voice and choice.

6. *A declaration can begin, resolve or end things*
    With declarations, you begin or open, you end or close and you resolve. Let us look at the following examples for each of these declarations:
    Declarations that begin or open:

    *   *The vision of our organization is....* The Board of Directors or the CEO may declare a (new) vision for the organization, and that opens a context for action by the employees of that organization.
    *   *You are now man and wife* is a declaration of a priest that begins a new relationship.
    *   *The target for this quarter for our team is...* targets also open up possibilities for new action.

    Declarations that resolve:

    *   When a judge passes his/her judgement, he/she is making a declaration that resolves a dispute, or passes a judgement of guilt or innocence.
    *   In cricket, when the umpire says 'Out or Not Out'— this is a declaration that resolves the dispute between two teams.
    *   'Yes/No' are also declarations that resolve.

    Declarations that end or close:

    *   'I'm sorry' is a common declaration that ends or closes a chapter. It provides completion, and an opportunity for a new opening.
    *   'Thank you' declares that I am satisfied and closes a cycle of commitment.
    *   'This relationship is over' is a declaration that ends a relationship.

There is power in what you say and it is important that you learn and start to exercise this power (Figure 5.1).

Figure 5.1 Elements of Declarations

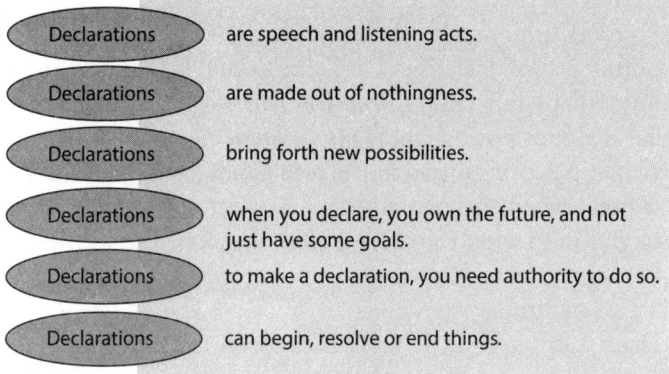

Declarations	are speech and listening acts.
Declarations	are made out of nothingness.
Declarations	bring forth new possibilities.
Declarations	when you declare, you own the future, and not just have some goals.
Declarations	to make a declaration, you need authority to do so.
Declarations	can begin, resolve or end things.

To Declare a Breakdown Is to Take a Stand

Many years back, I read a quotation somewhere that stated, 'If you don't stand for something, you will fall for everything'. When you declare a break, you take a stand for achieving a new future (we will talk about creating new futures in Chapter 8). And when you take a stand, interestingly, everything that is opposed to it arises. Every commitment or future that you as a leader articulate has the possibility of opposition, and you must be ready to face this opposition.

When I think of a stand, I am reminded of this image:

Source: Mitchell Krogg.[7]

The way I see this image is a lone tree standing in an empty barren land, facing the storm head-on. It is centred in the face of crises, with its roots firmly entrenched in the ground.

Another way of declaring that I take a stand is to state 'I commit to', and perhaps this comes from the battlefield analogy, where it may be stated for symbolic reasons for someone or a group to hold a particular piece of ground in the face of adversity. Generally, you take a stand when there is adversity or great opposition, and it is easy to give in to what you are not committed to. The way I see the above image, it seems easy for the tree to give up being a stand, in the face of a storm.

Martin Luther King Jr took a stand on the civil rights issue, Mahatma Gandhi took a stand for the independence of India, a coachee of mine took a stand for setting up a branch of his organization in the UK and my dear friend Sunil Jain has taken a stand for the differently abled to get equal opportunities in sports in India.

When you take a stand, you do not beat around the bush, you set aside your fear of mockery, scorn or laughter. You just make the choice and say it! And mean it. State it as if it is a fact, even if it isn't. If you want it to become a fact, you have to treat it like one. And you do not say 'you're sorry' when someone disagrees. You make it clear that this is the future you will take action inside of.

And you are an open invitation to others who want to join with you in making that future become real.

To Declare a Breakdown Is to Take Responsibility

The *Oxford Dictionary* has a number of definitions of the word 'responsible'.[8] It includes:

> Having an obligation to do something, or having control over or care for someone, as part of one's job or role; Having to report to (a superior) and be answerable to them for one's actions; Being the primary cause of something and so able to be blamed or credited for it.

We are going to focus on the meaning of 'responsible' that includes some of these orientations, but with the articulation: 'being responsible is to take the posture that you are the source or cause of something, you are open to be held accountable for the outcomes, you hold yourself accountable for the outcomes, and the outcomes can be shifted by your actions'.

What does it mean to take responsibility?

It is making the interpretation that when you assess something is not working, you will provide what is missing to make it work. This puts you in the posture of producing action, not waiting for someone else to take action. It puts you in the posture of being a leader. You may not know what to do, but in this posture, you will find out, or invent, what is needed. If you wait for others or act only if you know what to do, you become a victim and paralyze yourself with the reasons for your inaction and your lack of performance.

For example, you can take responsibility for your financial affairs, and act with 'ownership' that the outcomes are a product of your actions. To take the stand that you can impact, author and be accountable for the outcomes of actions is the fundamental posture of a leader, of an effective manager or executive.

We also have a choice to take responsibility for our promises and the promises of our teams; else we become just a part of the drift of action, not the author of them.

The opposite of responsibility is 'blame'. The Oxford Dictionary defines 'blame'[9] as '*Feel* or *declare* that (someone or something) is *responsible* for a *fault* or *wrong*; *Assign* the *responsibility* for a *bad* or *unfortunate situation* or *phenomenon* to (someone or something); *Responsibility* for a *fault* or *wrong*'.

From the earlier meaning of blame, we can create an articulation that blame is 'not taking responsibility, or not being at the source or the cause of something'. Blame is discharging pain; it is being helpless; it is saying that you are choosing *not* to be the cause of something; it is choosing inaction over action; it is hoping that someone somewhere will take action to change things. It is to surrender to a self-interpretation of impotence.

One major precondition to declaring a breakdown is *to be at the cause not at the effect*. You cannot declare a breakdown from the position of effect; in order to declare a breakdown, you must be the cause in the matter. If you are going to be at the effect, you can do nothing about the matter that concerns you and, in fact, will keep giving yourself excuses for not achieving the desired outcome.

A branch manager of a Swiss bank once said to me, 'I declare a breakdown in the recruitment of staff members for this new department we have planned. My new team of 5 members will join in the next 30 days. I will be the cause to make it happen. The only reason for me not achieving it would be if the recruitment team does not provide me good candidates to interview'.

This kind of a declaration is from the position of effect where he is giving the recruitment team the authority of deciding his future.

A lot of people claim to take a stand but do not really take a stand—they leave the back door open to exit. What this branch manager is doing is exactly that. On the face of it, he claims to be at the cause, and yet is at the effect of the recruitment team.

When you declare, you take a stand to be the cause for it, come what may. You are ready to be that tree in a barren land that does not falter despite the storm. You are centred[10] and have found your ground.[11] You do not give up when there is opposition, or lack of support. The branch manager here has a choice to work with the recruitment team, listen to their concerns and have a foolproof plan in place so that he attains his target. He then follows up to ensure that the plan is being executed. If not, he intervenes and does what is necessary to achieve what he has set out to achieve.

We often lead our lives as victims of circumstance. We allow ourselves to be overpowered by the situations and thoughts of people surrounding us. When you declare a breakdown, you do not allow this and resolve to be a stand.

John was a senior project manager in a multinational company. His team had a major project release lined up the following week. As usual, John was all pepped up and left no stone unturned to encourage his colleagues and motivate them to meet the deadlines. Yet, John saw that, despite their best efforts, they were not going to make it to the deadline. His junior managers and QA team lead washed their hands off saying they were doing the best they could do, and yet the project was going to miss the release deadline. At this stage, John had a choice. He declared a breakdown. He said that if things did not change, the release date would not be met. He asked himself, 'am I committed to my excuses or to the release date?'

It was an interesting question to ask, and it is the questions that you ask that are important. My claim is that answers get disclosed based on the questions that you ask. What you find is a function of what you look for. What you look for is what gets revealed to you. The answer that came up for John was that he was committed to the release date.

If he was committed to the release date and looking at how things were progressing—the release date would be missed—he needed to take new action. He spoke to another senior project manager in the organization and requested for two software developers for a week. John assured that senior project manager that in the future when he needed help, he would provide all the support required.

He spent late nights and early mornings briefing and working with the new software developers. He ensured that the project was released on the committed date.

John chose to be the cause of making the release happen on the committed date. He was at the source of making this happen. He chose responsibility over blame.

The Distinction Responsibility

Responsibility is being willing to be the cause in the matter!

Elements of Responsibility

- Choice
- Being the cause
- Care
- Taking a stand to find out what is missing.
- Taking actions despite not knowing how to

(*Continued*)

(*Continued*)

Conversation for Responsibility

   a.   What happens if I take no new action (Default future)?
   b.   What is my care? Am I OK with the default future?
   c.   If No, then what is the new future that I want to create?
   d.   Am I ready to take a stand to achieve that new future?

Pitfalls of not taking Responsibility

   a.   You end up becoming a victim
   b.   You are not taking care of your care
   c.   You lose out on leadership opportunities
   d.   It may impact the way people 'listen' to you.

Reflective Pause

In which areas of your life are you being the effect and not the cause? What is the impact of this on your cares, on your leadership and how people 'listen' to you?

You have a choice—do you want to take responsibility in these areas? What will it take for you to do so? What might be the costs of not doing so?

Please journal your thoughts.

No One Can Declare a Breakdown for You, You Have to Do It

So, when you do have the authority in your life, it is *you* who can declare and take charge of every situation in your life. When you say you are declaring a breakdown, you are saying you are taking a stand to achieve a future of design.

A declaration puts you in a posture to achieve that future. You are ready for actions and your body also resonates that feeling. There is a surge of energy within you when you declare, and that infectious energy propels your thoughts and actions towards making that declaration come alive. Without you having this energy, it most likely will not become available to others. You will not be able to coordinate with others for the new future.

You can declare breakdowns in the achievement of your targets, your relationship with your colleagues, the completion of your project on schedule, your plan to travel to Europe by the year end or anything else that matters to you.

If you are leading a strained relationship with your wife and the inevitable future of you separating with your wife is not what appeals to you, then you have a choice to declare a breakdown. The moment you decide that you will take a stand and are committed to regaining peace and love in your life, you will do whatever it takes to attain it.

All of this can happen only when you choose to declare a breakdown. No one can declare a breakdown for you.

When Sonam came to me, she was desperate. In her quest to find someone to help her husband, Ashish, she realized she was the one who could benefit from coaching and would be able to steer her husband back on track. Ashish had been doing pretty well in the corporate world. He had been very successfully 'climbing the corporate ladder' so to say, and had a whole bunch of accolades to show. His two kids went to an international private school and Sonam was doing reasonably well too as a lecturer in a renowned university. Of late, however, he was losing interest in his work.

He suddenly realized he had not enjoyed his life and had spent most of his younger days trying to earn money and compete to reach a senior position. So now he was always trying to find reasons to be away from work. He bought himself a boat and would sail away for days alone. He started indulging himself in luxury and even bought himself a fancy car. He was spending more than what was prudent, given their financial standards.

Sonam saw what was coming but was unable to have a decent conversation with Ashish without him becoming defensive and blowing his top off. With coaching, Sonam realized she herself had not committed to being a stand to resolve their economic crisis. She saw that she had been constantly bickering and nagging him about his spending ways and was totally missing what was concerning him.

After a few sessions of our conversations, she spoke to him again and showed him that the financial situation they were in would not be resolved if both of them did not work towards resolution. She said she was committed to getting things sorted and would take on extra classes at college or even accept invitations for weekend lectures if need be. Ashish did not pay heed to her and was too engrossed, wanting to live for himself. Soon enough he had spent more than he had earned and had a whole string of debts attached for the next 5 years.

Sonam was committed to being a stand and started working very hard towards it; but single-handedly what she was accomplishing was minuscule compared to what they desperately needed that moment in their economic condition. She was fighting a lonely and losing battle.

But she did not give up, and she continued her conversations with him, and one day when his credit card company blocked his card due to extravagant purchases and poor repayment, Ashish received a jolt. He now saw what Sonam was saying all along. This was when Ashish was ready to be coached.

Sonam could not declare a breakdown for Ashish. Ashish had to declare his own breakdown. When he declared the breakdown, he was committed to creating a new future. *Creating a new future* is what we will discuss in Chapter 8.

Team Breakdowns

The First Question to Be Asked Is 'What Is a Team'?

A team is a group of people that share a promise.[12] A team is constituted by the shared promise. Without a shared promise, the team is not a team; it is just a group of people together. Teamwork, whether it is effective or not, is generated by the conversations of the team members. The culture of your team is evidenced in the kind of conversations you have and the results that they produce.

Our interpretation at IGL is that a team exists to fulfil a promise, and the team members having the same shared promise is what constitutes, or brings into existence, the team itself. To be effective, the team has to take action to fulfil its promise, produce satisfaction for the team's customers and team members and effectively address all the aspects of shared action that a team must engage in.

A team exists to make a bigger promise that one person alone cannot fulfil.

Effective Teams

Effective teams are those that engage in and are capable of having the conversations that produce the necessary commitments for successful coordination of action. Effective teams have a clear understanding of what these conversations are and how to have them. The topic of this book is not all types of team conversations, and so we are focusing only on the 'declaring a breakdown' conversation.

Declaring Team Breakdowns

In a team, it is important that everybody on the team involved declares appropriate breakdowns. If achievement of promises is in jeopardy, it is essential that everybody declares a breakdown or is committed to the team breakdown, so that they are all aligned with their overall commitment of the team. If only one person declares a breakdown, then he/she is the lone one dreaming a future for the entire team and everyone involved in the process.

If team members take ownership for the commitments of the team, and can 'see' the default future of their actions, which is that the team will not meet its commitment to the team's customer—then any team member can declare a breakdown. For it to be a team breakdown, the team member declaring a breakdown needs to generate a commitment from all team members to declaring the breakdown.

I recently conducted a 6-month training programme for a software product company headquartered in Houston, Texas. I was working with the Senior Director of Customer Support along with his management team. Their team's customer satisfaction score was 82 per cent when they started out with the programme. At the start of the programme, as the leader of the team, the Senior Director declared a breakdown. He stated that if no new action was taken, the customer satisfaction score would remain at 82 per cent, or even go down. He declared that he wanted this score to be 87 per cent before the end of the 6-month programme.

This declaration created an interruption in the flow of the way the team operated. If others in the team accepted this declaration, they would have to change the way they functioned. It would mean getting out of their old practices, and creating new practices—those that served the organization better.

When the Senior Director shared this with his team, the entire management team committed to this future. His management team in turn solicited commitment from their subordinates. The entire business unit of over 250 employees committed to this future. Once they had this commitment, the management team of this business unit then designed actions so that this future could be achieved.

What is interesting to note here is that within 4 months itself the team achieved this future. Had the leader not declared this breakdown, and each member of the team not owned the breakdown, chances are the team would still be at 82 per cent customer satisfaction scores.

Summary and Reconstruction of Our Understanding

1. Care is fundamental to declaring breakdowns. It is important to be clear on 'what is it that you care for' and 'are you taking care of your care'. If not, you have the choice of declaring a breakdown.

2. Declarations are a powerful speech and listening act, and here are elements of the distinction declaration:

   a. Declarations are made out of nothingness.
   b. Declarations bring forth new possibilities.
   c. When you declare, you own the future and not just have some goals.
   d. To make a declaration, you need authority to do so.
   e. Declarations can begin, resolve or end things.

3. Declarations bring forth a new future into existence. This new future gets created in the speaking of someone. Till such a time, this new future did not exist. It came into existence only through the act of speaking.

4. In a declaration, your word comes before the world, that is, you first create your future in your word and then the world gets created.

5. Experience lies in the past, and to rely on the past to declare a new future may be a mistake. People believe they have 'experience' and that 'experience' tells them what is possible. This view of life is constraining. It is likely to repeat the past instead of opening a new future.

6. Using experience to declare a future may be constraining; however, once you have declared a future, your experience will be of immense use to you in taking actions to achieve that future.

7. Leadership is about having authority in a community to make certain declarations that brings something into existence by the saying of it. When a person is not authorized by a community or granted authority, then a declaration will not be effective.

8. A key question is, 'Who has authority in the matter of your life?' In the matter of your life, the authority to make declarations rests with you. You have the authority in the matter of your own life. It may be that you very easily give away this authority to your parents, children, bosses, clients, juniors, friends and, at times, even to random people.

9. While you certainly have authority in the matter of your life, the next question is, 'Do you give yourself this authority in the matter of your life?'

10. 'Why do you have authority in the matter of your own life?' The answer is 'Because you say so!' It is as simple as that. You even declare that you have authority in the matter of your life.

11. To take responsibility is to take the posture that you are the source or cause of something, and the outcomes can be shifted by your actions. It is making the interpretation that when you assess something is not working, you will

provide what is missing to make it work. This puts you in the posture of producing action, not waiting for action. It puts you in the posture of being a leader. You may not know what to do, but in this posture, you will find out, or invent, what is needed. If you wait for others or act only if you know what to do, you become a victim and paralyse yourself with the reasons for your inaction and your lack of performance.

12. Blame on the other hand is 'not taking responsibility, or not being at the source or the cause of something'. Blame is discharging pain; it is being helpless; it is saying that you are choosing *not* to be the cause of something; it is choosing inaction over action; it is hoping that someone somewhere will take action to change things.

13. One major precondition to declare a breakdown is *to be at the cause not at the effect*. You cannot declare a breakdown from the position of effect; in order to declare a breakdown, you must be the cause in the matter. If you are going to be at the effect, you can do nothing about the matter that concerns you and, in fact, will keep giving yourself excuses for not achieving the desired outcome.

14. We often lead our lives as victims of circumstance. We allow ourselves to be overpowered by the situations and thoughts of people surrounding us. Declaring a breakdown does not have power until you resolve to be a stand.

15. An interesting question to ask yourself: 'Are you committed to your excuses or are you committed to your results?' It is the questions that you ask that are important. My claim is that answers get disclosed based on the questions that you ask. What you find is a function of what you look for. What you look for is what gets revealed to you.

16. Only you can choose to declare a breakdown. No one can declare a breakdown for you. When the team leader declares a breakdown, you have to choose to own the breakdown as a team member.

Generative Practices

1. Reflect on what you care about. Write down in your journal what you declare to be your key cares or concerns in life.
2. For each concern, assess whether you are satisfied with how you are taking care of this concern.
3. What are the missing declarations that you can make in each area of your care?
4. Do you choose to be a stand and take responsibility for achieving the future that you have declared in each of your cares? If so, what could be the missing actions to achieve the future that you have declared? As you read the book, these missing actions will start to open up for you—we also have a dedicated chapter on missing actions. However, at this stage, we request you to speculate about these missing actions.
5. Is your team constituted in a shared promise? If not, what could be the shared promise of your team? And what would you need to do to get others to commit to a shared promise of your team?
6. If your team is already committed to a shared promise, consider declaring a breakdown every time the team promise is at threat or at risk.
7. Journal your thoughts and practices. Make at least one entry a day as part of your practice to create possibilities in your life and work.

Notes

1. Chalmers Brothers, *Language and the Pursuit of Happiness* (Florida: New Possibilities Press, 2005).
2. From unpublished papers written by Bob Dunham for the Generative Leadership programme of IGL.
3. Ibid.
4. Mathew Budd and Larry Rothstein, *You Are What You Say You Are* (New York: Three Rivers Press, 2000).

5. http://india.gov.in/sites/upload_files/npi/files/coi_part_full.pdf, accessed 16 February 2016.

6. Steven D. Levitt and Stephen J. Dubner, *Think Like a Freak* (USA: William Morrow, an imprint of Harper Collins, 2014).

7. Mitchell Krog Photography: http://mitchellkrog.com

8. http://www.oxforddictionaries.com/definition/english/responsible?q=Responsible&searchDictCode=all, accessed 16 February 2016.

9. http://www.oxforddictionaries.com/definition/english/blame, accessed 16 February 2016.

10. Being centred is being in a physical, mental and emotional state of choice. We are centred when our body, mind and emotions are in a state where we can choose our actions. When we are not in a state to choose our actions, we are 'off-centre'; our reactions and tendencies choose for us. We cannot blend when we are off-centre. In centring, we attain complete balance and focus regardless of our situations:

- Our mind is alert, we are connected to what we care about and we are free of distracting mental chatter.
- Our mood is serene and open to the current situation.
- Our physical state is dynamically relaxed, alert, balanced around our centre of gravity and ready for action.

These three aspects are mutually connected.

11. To find your ground when making declarations is that you can trust your declaration. You are operating from a position of certainty, rather than of disbelief or hesitation.

12. Bob Dunham has a yet unpublished paper called the 'Ten Conversations of Teams'. I came across this paper in my education at IGL, USA. I have referred to the above-mentioned paper in this section.

6

Get Present to 'What Is So' (Assertions)

The second step after you declare a breakdown is to get clear about or present to 'what actually happened' or 'what is so'. Once you declare a breakdown, you then start with distinguishing between 'what is so' and 'what you make of what is so'.

'What is so' is the realm of assertions. 'What I make of what is so' refers to the assessments or judgements that you create automatically and, most times, subconsciously.

Speech and Listening Act: Assertions or 'What Is So'

An assertion is a claim of fact, which is either true or false, to a standard established by the community.

Assertions can be substantiated or refuted through observation and evidence (Figure 6.1).

Speech and Listening Act: Assessments or 'What I Make of What Is So'

An assessment is a statement of evaluation, opinion or judgement. Assessments are neither true nor false. Instead, they can be grounded (supported by evidence) or ungrounded (Figure 6.2).

Figure 6.1   The Important Elements of Assertions

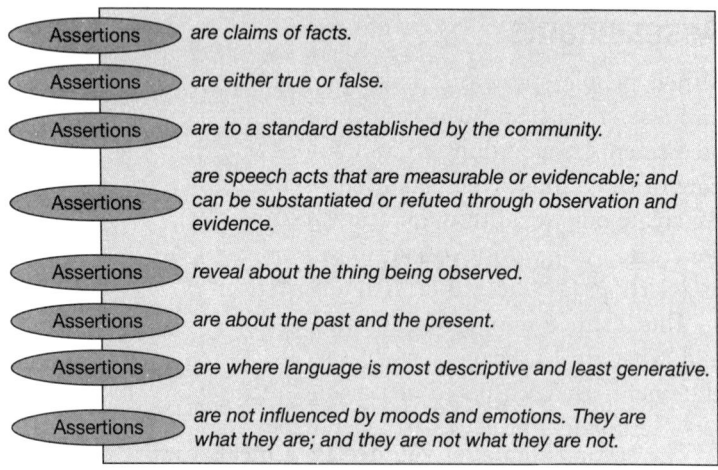

Figure 6.2   The Important Elements of Assessments

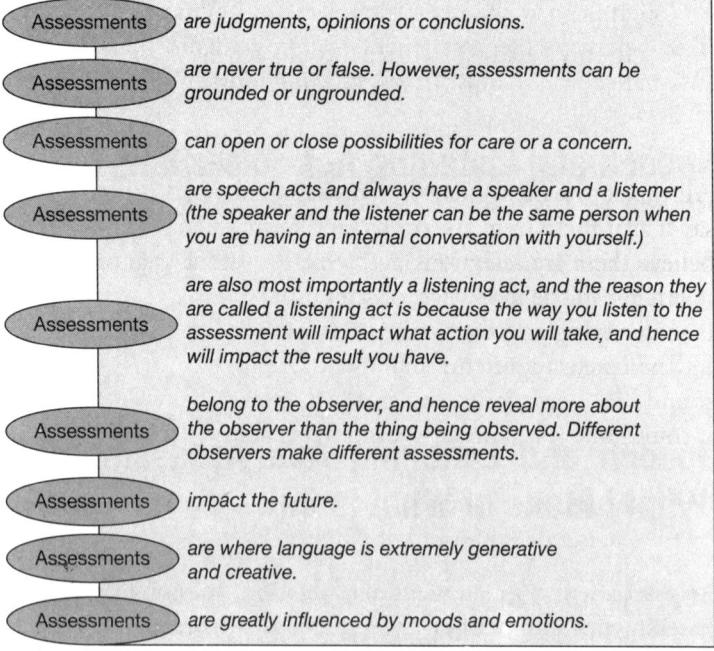

A Comparison of Assertions and Assessments

When people speak or think, they confuse between assertions and assessments, and it is very common for people to hold their assessments as assertions, their opinions as facts. This is where the core of the difficulty lies. As I have stated in the earlier chapters, we create our world through our assessments, and then we forget we created this world—because we start to hold our assessments as assertions, as true, rather than perspectives and judgements.

This distinction of assertions and assessments, or of 'what is so' and 'what am I making of what is so', is critical. There are various statements that we make in passing, and without noticing, that have an impact in the way we operate our lives, such as

- 'I cannot do this',
- 'This is an impossible target',
- 'The only way I can succeed is by doing this and this…',
- 'This is a daunting task',
- 'If only I had (this), then I could achieve (that)',
- 'I am not a morning person' and
- 'She is so annoying'.

All the above-mentioned statements are assessments, and yet we say it as if these were assertions (and more importantly, we start to believe these are assertions).

To get a little more rigorous, let us take this last statement 'She is so annoying' and discuss it.

The construct of this statement 'She is so annoying' makes it sound like 'being annoying' is a fact about that person. We make it sound like it is similar to other facts about her, such as,

- she is 5 feet 8 inches,
- she is a daughter of her parents,
- she is a sister of 2 brothers,
- she is a mother of 1 son and
- she is the general manager of a bank.

The above-mentioned statements can be claimed to be facts about her. Assertions are not dependent on the observer, and irrespective of who the observer is, the above-mentioned statements remain as assertions.

However, when you say 'She is so annoying', you say it like an assertion, which is like a claim of fact. It is almost like saying 'She is 5 feet 8 inches tall'.

Both these sentences begin with 'She is _____', making what comes after 'she is' a fact about that person. These sentences have been constructed similarly, yet being 5 feet 8 inches is indeed a fact, and being annoying is not a fact; it is your assessment of that person.

When you say 'She is so annoying', you are actually saying 'Given the observer I am, right now in this moment, I assess this person to be annoying'.

When you say it this way, you are now saying that annoying is not a property of hers. You are saying that it is *you* who assesses her as annoying in that moment and that you may change your assessment of her at a later date and time.

It is imperative to distinguish the distinctions between assertion and assessment and recognize that one is a claim of fact and that the other is just an opinion. Most often, we mix these up, and not create a distinction between these two distinctions.

Let us see a comparison between assertions and assessments.

Assertions	Assessments

Assertions are claims of facts.
    For example: *Ram is the Managing Director of AAA Corporation.*
	Assessments are opinions, judgments or subjective statements.
	    For example: *Ram is brilliant at his work.*

Assertions belong to the thing being observed.
    For example: *Ram is the CEO of AAA Corporation.*
Here you are speaking about Ram's designation and the organization he works for.
	Assessments belong to the Observer. Different Observers will have different opinions. (Even if a group observers the thing in a particular way, the assessment still belongs to the group and not to the thing being observed. It becomes a group assessment.)
	    For example: *Ram is brilliant at work is your* assessment of Ram. There may be others who may not make the same assessment as you.

Assertions	Assessments
Assertions can either be true or false. For example: *Rohit came late for yesterday's meeting by 30 minutes.* If there was a camera recording the meeting, it could be proved whether or not Rohit came late or not.	Assessments cannot be verified to be true or false. However, assessments can be grounded or ungrounded. For example: *Rohit is unreliable.* Rohit being unreliable cannot be generalized and cannot be proved true or false. However, you can give evidence of Rohit coming late for all meetings and hence you make a grounded assessment that Rohit is unreliable as far as coming on time for these meetings is concerned.
Assertions reveal about the thing being observed For example: *John did not wish Peter or Anna 'Good morning' on Monday morning.*	Assessments reveal more about the observer/ the standards of the observer than the thing being observed. For example: *Peter assesses John to be rude because he did not wish him good morning.* So, as per Peter's standard, that is being rude. John did not wish Anna 'good morning' too and as per Anna that does not mean John is rude.
Assertions have to do with the past and the present. For example: *In yesterday's meeting Ram came late by 30 minutes.*	Assessments have everything to do with the future. For example: *Ram is unreliable, and once you assess someone as unreliable, in the future you relate to that person as unreliable.*
Assertions are where language is most descriptive and least generative (the only speech act where language is descriptive). For example: *The dinner table is 10 feet by 4 feet.* In this case I am describing a property of the table.	Assessments are where language is extremely generative and creative. For example: *The table is big and we can play table tennis on it.* In my language, I have created the dining table to be a table tennis table and also big enough to play table tennis on it.
Assertions are not influenced by moods and emotions. For example: *A stranger's elbow touches Chris.*	Assessments are greatly influenced by moods and emotions. For example: *In an angry mood, Chris assesses that the stranger 'should be keeping a safe distance' and yells at the stranger for not maintaining the distance. In a happy mood, Chris makes the assessment 'it's OK—it's a mistake' and smiles at the stranger.*
Assertions are 'what is so'. For example: *The table is 10 feet by 4 feet.*	Assessments are 'what you make of what is so'. For example: *I make this table big enough to play table tennis on it.*

Let us see some examples of assertions and assessments.

Assertions (What Is So)	Assessments (What I Make of What Is So)
Peter came 1 hour late to work.	Peter is not a disciplined manager.
My car had an accident.	I am now going to be inconvenienced and will find it difficult to get to work.
John dropped the bottle.	John is clumsy.
Susan's height is 5 feet 10 inches.	Susan is a tall lady.
The temperature is 10 degrees Celsius today.	It is cold today.
Karen to Angelica: 'Your target for this quarter is $2 million'.	Angelica in her thoughts makes the assessment: 'This is impossible'.
I forgot my lines on stage.	I am shy that is why I forgot my lines on stage.
Husband to wife: 'Where is my book?'	Wife thinks, 'You are so disorganized'.
Angelina did not complete the project on schedule.	Angelina is incompetent.

There are innumerable events that take place in our everyday lives. We as humans by default pick and choose certain events and create our interpretations or assessments around the events. In simpler words, we humans are story-making machines. When an event occurs, we very quickly generate a story about it in our minds, and one of the traps we easily fall into is believing that this story is 'the truth'.

Worse, we fail to recognize that we made up that 'truth'.

Let us see a typical day for Alan at work. Alan is the Senior Manager of a multinational bank. On one Friday, he enters his office premises totally engrossed in checking his emails on his phone. He does however hear the security man greeting and wishing 'good morning' to his colleague who is walking along with him. The security man does not greet Alan. Alan in that moment, very subconsciously, assesses that the security guy does not respect him. He gives an angry glance to the security man.

What was so (assertion): *The security man wished the other manager 'good morning'.*

What did Alan make of what was so (assessment): *The security guy does not respect me.*

Alan goes towards his office, brushing off the seemingly unpleasant incident. At the coffee station, he sees two women employees speaking to each other. In that moment, he makes an assessment in his head: 'The weekend for them has already begun and that they are wasting their productive office time'. He just shakes his head, makes a mental note about another point he needs to discuss in his weekly staff meeting about unproductivity and moves on.

What was so (assertion): *Two employees talking next to the coffee station.*

What did Alan make of what was so (assessment): *The weekend for them has already begun and that they are wasting their productive office time.*

And the day continues.

This book is not about a hypothetical example of Alan. This book is for and about you. My claim is that human beings operate like I have described Alan earlier.

An event takes place (what is so).
Human beings create a story, about what is so,
hold the story to be the truth and
forget that they created this truth.

They then live their lives operating inside of a truth that they have created, having completely forgotten that they are the authors of these stories. They are empowered by these stories, and sometimes, they are disempowered by these stories. They become happy, sad, angry, frustrated, resigned, resentful and so forth, all because of the stories that they create.

Reflective Pause

At this stage, I invite you to take a reflect pause and consider the stories you are creating and holding to be the truth.

The Importance of Assessments

In my workshops, when I distinguish between assertions and assessments, people start to make a story that assessments are not important and that assessments should not be made. I have not stated that, nor have I implied that anywhere. On the contrary, assessments are very important to make.

Assertions are facts, and they do not have a meaning separate from 'this is so'. By themselves, none of these statements of assertions mean anything in particular:

- Peter came 1 hour late to work.
- John dropped the bottle.
- Your target for the quarter is $2 million.

The meaning in these statements is through the assessments that you make. You are the author who creates this meaning: One observer, based on the above-mentioned assertions, can make the following assessments:

- Peter is not a disciplined manager.
- John is clumsy.
- This target is impossible.

Another observer may make a completely different set of assessments based on the same above set of assertions. Different observers will make different meanings.

Assertions do not produce actions. As I have mentioned earlier, by and of themselves, assertions do not mean anything in particular. The actions you take are governed by the assessments you make.

If the results are a function of the actions you take, and actions are a function of the assessments you make—then if you really want results, you need to question the assessments you are making. People are so often consumed by actions to get results that they do not even question the source of their actions (Figure 6.3).

Figure 6.3   The Relationship Between Assessments, Actions and Results

Cedrick: The Star Performer

Vivek, a Delivery Head in an IT organization and one of my coachees, assessed that the employees in his unit were disgruntled and their productivity low. His commitment was to have happy and satisfied employees. One of the issues that came to the forefront in our conversations was that he did not trust his employees.

He quoted an example, saying:

> Cedrick is one of the star performers in my team but only when he wants to be. I find him lacking commitment to the work and does not think twice before taking an unscheduled leave. When he is in a good mood to work he goes on a rampage and his work outweighs that of 3 employees put together. Last week he called in sick and I threw a fit of rage, because that was just a week before a major software release for my team and a project that we had been working on for more than a year. I was curt with him on the phone and was almost about to throw verbal abuses at him when I stopped short. I had been counting on him to come and make up for the backlog in the deadlines.

On further probing, Vivek continued:

> When Cedrick called in for a leave, I felt my teeth clenching, my eyes became fixated, I think I was also taking shorter breaths. My mind went in a whirlwind of thoughts. The first thought that came to me was about our project release and the

impending disaster if the deadline was not met, the unhappy and upset clients, the barrage of angry emails, the late night work and more flashed in front of me in a matter of seconds.

But the image that made me the angriest was when I visualized him in a movie theatre and that scene did not go well in keeping my temperament calm. Actually, in my younger days I had 'bunked' college and office a lot for such reasons and I assume that's what my employees are doing too. I mean, after all, if you are committed how can a cold or cough keep you away from work. That whole day I was extremely irritated with all that happened and ended up screaming at my other reportees, all because of Cedrick. The next day when Cedrick reported to work, I blasted him for being absent the previous day and ensured he worked to make good the loss of productivity his absence had caused.

Let us diagnose this example closely.

Assertion about the event	Cedrick called in sick
Assessment by Vivek (What he made of what is so)	• Cedrick is not sick and is watching a movie, and due to his absence, the deadlines will not be met • There was an impending disaster • The clients would be unhappy and upset • He would receive a barrage of angry emails • He and his team would have to work late at night to catch up
Actions	Reprimanding Cedrick and making him work doubly hard the next day
Mood	Irritated throughout the day
Result	Unhappy employees (Cedrick and the others that he screamed at)

Keeping the same above-mentioned assertion, Vivek could have made many different assessments. Let us see what the impact would be if he had made a different assessment.

Assertion about the event	Cedrick called in sick
Another assessment that could be made by Vivek (What he made of what is so)	Cedrick is indeed sick
Mood this acceptance could give him	Renewed energy and commitment to meet the deadline
Some other actions that he could take	• Call a meeting of all other reportees • Speak to them about his fear of the deadline not being met • Get a recommitment/buy-in from them to work towards achieving the deadline • Check if there is an employee from other teams free to help them • If his technical expertise permitted, he could himself have been hands-on
Result	Probably a deadline that was met and employees with renewed sense of trust in their boss

Naomi and Her Child

Naomi is a dedicated mother. She goes out of her way to ensure her young 7-year-old son gets the best of everything. One day when her son refuses to accept an invitation from his teacher to tell a story in front of the class in school, Naomi's mind starts churning up a story that if her child does not speak up in front of the class, he will get lower marks on his tests, his teacher will think little of him, his friends may not relate to him, he will lose his confidence and he will turn into a shy boy!

These stories led her to scold her son, who did not understand why his otherwise calm mother was getting all hyper over an issue that was trivial in his world!

Assertion about the event (What is so)	Child refused to tell a story in front of the class
Assessment that was made by Naomi (What she made of what is so)	Her son will get lower marks on his tests, his teacher will think little of him, his friends may not relate to him, he will lose his confidence and he will turn into a shy boy!
Actions	Naomi scolded her child
Result	An unhappy and confused 7-year-old boy

Naomi could have made any number of different assessments. Let us look at what would have happened had she formed a different assessment.

Assertion about the event	Child refused to tell a story in front of the class
Another assessment that could be made by Naomi (What she made of what is so)	• He is a child, he will learn as he grows • He probably did not understand what his teacher meant • He is not confident about the topic he needs to speak on • He needs more practise
Some other actions that she could take	• Let it be and allow her child that space to learn and grow • Speak calmly to her child and help him understand what it means to speak in front of the class • Give him instances where she herself had broken her barrier of speaking in front of an audience, thus reinstating an element of self-confidence in the child • Speak to her child and explain to him the topic that needs to be spoken on and make the entire conversation more visual and exciting for the child
Results	A happy, confident child (which is Naomi's ultimate commitment)

My Shyness Runs My Life

'My problem is I am shy,' said a coachee of mine in one of my sessions. He is Tanvir, a Senior Director in a global software development firm. He quoted saying:

I do not like to speak out in front of an audience; I prefer to keep to myself whether it is at home or at the office. My wife also has this constant complaint against me that I am too non-verbal. She sometimes thinks I don't have emotions! I can't help it; I have been like this for a long time. I realise this shyness is keeping me away from a lot of things I could probably achieve or could have already achieved in life. I was too shy to go up and tell my boss that I wanted to work on a particular project and that I had the skill sets to achieve the desired results. I thought I would be playing my own trumpet so I kept quiet. Eventually the project was handed over to someone else and I just sat back and let it pass.

I am too shy to tell my children how much I love them, I don't want them to think I am an emotional person. I want them to see me as a strong and strict father. But now I think they have distanced themselves from me and I think it could be because I shy away from communicating my love. But I can't help it I am shy!

Tanvir was blaming his shyness for the missed–achievements in his life. He was not being the cause to turn events in his favour. He was operating in his comfort zone (*it is comfortable to state 'I am shy', and then not do anything because of this shyness*), and led his life without taking the responsibility of creating a future of choice.

I saw Tanvir ready to break out of his story of shyness. The very fact that he had even spoken about it showed that he wanted freedom from this story. I asked him when was the first time that he discovered he was shy. He mentioned that this was during his junior college days. He had participated in a play and when he went up on stage, he forgot all his lines. The play flopped because of him. He said, 'That's when I realized I am shy'.

I asked him, 'You are shy—is this statement an assertion or an assessment?' He looked confused. He said, 'This seems like an assessment, but it is true'.

Can you see how people once they make an assessment hold on to the assessment so dearly? Tanvir was not ready to let go of this assessment, and had made this 'the truth'. He had lived in this assessment for so long, he felt insecure without this assessment.

Tanvir had reached the position of being a senior director in a global software development firm; I asked him, 'To reach this position, you may have had to make some bold moves?'

Back came his response, 'Oh yeah, of course!'

I looked at him with a smile, and he realized where I was coming from. It looked like something had shifted for him in that moment. He was not shy; he had been bold on many occasions. It is just that he was operating as shy where it suited him.

'I am shy' is a common story I have noticed that people have about themselves. This is only *a story, an assessment,* and is not an assertion. This is their truth inside of which they have lived their life. Tanvir spent 20 years living inside of *this story.*

Once this new awareness had dawned upon Tanvir, he decided that he would not play the blame game anymore and would work around his conversations that were restricting him. With practice, Tanvir started catching himself making up stories about events and people. Often, he caught himself stopping from approaching a person or speaking up due to his own assessments about the situation or people.

One day, he excitedly and unexpectedly called me and said:

I have always wanted to have a word with the Global CEO of my organisation. I would meet him briefly during meetings but always was too shy to go up to him and speak, but today I just stopped the thoughts in my head about what he would think about me and sent him an email that I would like to speak to him. To my surprise, he responded back and requested me to join him for coffee break a few days later. I have just returned from having a one hour coffee meeting with him! A whole new bunch of possibilities have opened up for me after this conversation.

And all it took was to break the self-imposed barriers created by the assessments made by Tanvir about himself.

Reflective Pause

What are the assessments that you have about yourself that are stopping you from breaking through. What are the assessments that you have about others? What is the impact these assessments have on *your* results?

Get present to these stories.

Grounded Assessments

We usually do not make assessments about our assessments. We just have assessments and leap forward with our overwhelming opinion and action. But when something important is at stake, we will produce better results if we ask the question 'Is this the best assessment for me to make given what I care about, and the importance of the consequence of my choice?'

While distinguishing assertions and assessments earlier, I had stated that assertions are claims of facts and are either true or false; and assessments are opinions, judgements or conclusions and are not true or false but grounded or ungrounded.

I have also stated the importance of making assessments. If you do not make assessments, you will not take action. To take action, you need to make assessments. So, how do you know which assessments are grounded and which ones are not grounded? Which assessments you can trust and which you cannot trust? Which assessments will serve you better?

Grounded assessments are assessments that have answered a set of questions that require clarification before the listener can accept the assessment. These questions concern care, standards, domain and evidence.

Grounding is a practice to make assessments about assessments. If an assessment is 'grounded', then it has evidence to an acceptable standard and is more likely to be effective in producing a desired outcome than an assessment that is 'ungrounded'—lacking clear standards, evidence or specification of the domain of concern. Grounding does not make an assessment true; it only provides evidence and argument that it is a good assessment for our purpose. And ungrounded assessments only mean the assessments lack a relevant story with evidence to trust the assessments. In grounding, we recommend that you ask certain questions. We ask that you seek for rigorous answers, and use the answers to generate the assessment about the assessment.

Figure 6.4   Grounding of Assessments

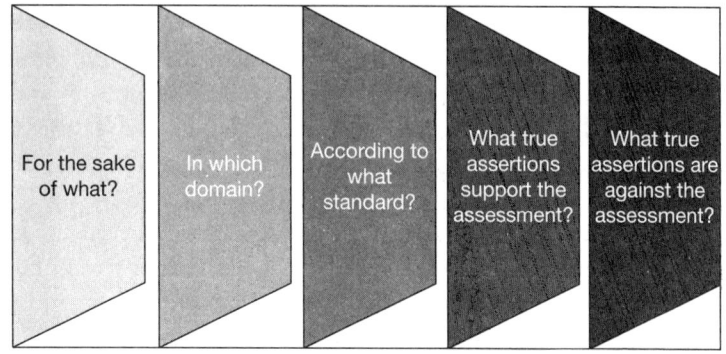

To ground assessments, we find answers to the following questions (Figure 6.4):

- *For the sake of what?*

  When you start to observe your assessments, my claim is that a lot of your automatic assessments will not pass this first test of grounding assessments: 'For the sake of what are you making this assessment?' You will see that a lot of assessments are being made for no real reason or future action, and yet assessments go and sit in the future, impacting how you look at another person, yourself or, for that matter, the situation at hand.

- *In which domain?*

  Humans are story (assessment) making machines. They make a story and forget the domain in which they made the story or the assessment. For example, if you write a test of mathematics and do not get passing marks, you would have failed to pass the mathematics test. The domain in which you failed was mathematics. But the assessment you make is 'I am a failure'.

- *According to what standard?*

  It is important to identify the standard based on which you are making the assessment. I was delivering a workshop for a company headquartered in Israel, and the leadership of a business unit (BU) was discussing the reporting structure in that organization. They were talking about how their immediate boss, the head of the BU had a different standard of quality and how the CEO had a completely different standard. So, the products that were being developed were of an acceptable standard of the BU Head, but were not good enough as per the standard of the CEO. The BU Head and the CEO did not share the same standards.

- *What true assertions support the assessment?*
  Assessments have to be based on assertions. However, if you observe, many of your assessments are based on other assessments, making your assessments ungrounded. To ground your assessments, see if there are any true assertions that support the assessment.
- *What true assertions are against the assessment?*
  As an extension of the previous point, what are the true assertions that argue against the assessment? This will help you make a grounded assessment.

So, in general, grounding is a way to produce more trust in an assessment. As a matter of fact, the whole idea of grounding an assessment is so that you can trust your assessment, and base your actions on this assessment. What is important to note is that when you have grounded your assessment, your assessment is still only your assessment. It does not become an assertion. Others may not accept your grounding because they may have selected a different domain, a different standard, different assertions to support or not support the assessment or may even have a different purpose. The point is not just to 'ground', but to design the grounding categories that are most valuable for what is cared about.

We have an exception to this, a related concern, and a major opportunity. The exception is that people with high degrees of competence, virtuosity or mastery may not be able to 'ground' their assessments explicitly—this is because they have actually developed a sense of intuition and sensibility that goes beyond a logical argument. However, they will have a track record of accomplishment that allows others to formulate a grounding argument of why their intuition should be trusted. Grounding still applies, but from another observer. The responsibility for grounding (assessing the assessment) in this case goes from the speaker to the listener, or to the person evaluating whether to trust their assessment.

Where Do Our Assessments Come From?

Our automatic assessments come from our personal history, from our culture and from our practices. Culture refers to standard and habitual actions, behaviours and attitudes that arise from a background of shared interpretations, standards, values and standard practices of an organization or community. People coming from one culture and historical background may make one set of assessments, while people from another culture or historical background may make a completely different set of assessments about the same situation.

For example, Jai, coming from an organization culture of wearing jeans and casuals at work and moving to another organization where formals was the common unwritten dress code, assessed this new organization he joined as being *stuck up and interested in non-essentials, rather than the quality of work the person delivers.*

Similarly, Marshall moved from an organization that had a formal dress code to an organization where employees could wear what they liked, and most employees came to work in casuals. Marshall assessed his new place of work to be *too casual* and *unprofessional* (for him formal wear was a sign of professionalism).

Like culture, people make assessments based on their historical practices. A practice is a standard set of actions that are engaged to take care of recurrent situations. People have practised making the kind of assessments they make. It has happened for so long, it has now become the truth for them.

Acceptance

Acceptance is a critical distinction when declaring breakdowns. My experience has been that people accept 'their assessments' as the truth, and move forward with the declarations. This is a fundamental error commonly made by working executives. To make a declaration, you have to distinguish 'what is so' from 'what am I making of what is so'. And then accept 'what is so' for what it is.

Acceptance is acknowledging 'what is so'. It is acknowledging the facts about events. Most times, we accept our assessments about the situations to be the truth. We accept that meetings are boring; we accept a certain boss is tough; we accept our targets are impossible to meet. This is *not* acceptance. These are all assessments. You do not accept assessments; you accept assertions.

'What is so' *is* what is so in this moment, and in this moment, you have no choice in this matter (right now, the amount of money you have or do not have; right now, you have been declined for the promotion or raise; right now, your weight is 100 kg; and so forth). Acceptance is acknowledging this.

It is not acknowledging that I am poor and will never have enough money, or I am not good enough, or I am fat and will remain like this forever.

In acceptance, we are grounded both somatically[1] in our bodies and in our assessments. Our acceptance *includes* our ambitions. We accept that we have ambitions, and we move from our ambitions in the world as it shows up.

Acceptance does not mean agreement or approval. It means we accept the assertions of the situation as our starting point.

When declaring breakdowns, you *accept* the assertions or 'what it so', and are ready for action inside of your commitment.

Here are some important elements of 'acceptance':

- Acceptance is acknowledging *what is*. Acceptance is *not* acknowledging your assessments as 'the Truth'.
- Acceptance means that we are centred in the world *as it is* and ready for action, rather than consumed and off-centre with our *assessments or preferences about the situation*.
- We are *present*, and can take action, rather than being in our mood and conversations.
- We are in the mood of 'it is the way it is—now what am I committed to, and what actions will I take to fulfil my commitments?' rather than the mood of 'I don't like the way it is, and I'm going to be triggered and perturbed'.
- Acceptance has a lot to do with letting go of assessments.
- Acceptance is not agreement or preference; it is the mood of being open to 'what is' and starting from there for a path to the future, rather than being in reaction to 'what is' with assessment and moods.[2]

Reflective Pause

Take a few moments of a reflective pause.

1. If you are disempowered about something, distinguish the assertion and 'accept' the assertions.
2. Identify areas in your like where you are showing up accepting 'assessments' of yours.

Presence

To declare breakdowns, as discussed earlier, you need to accept the assertions as they are. The concern we have is people do not distinguish between assertions and assessments, and end up accepting their assessments as the truth.

To *accept* the assertions, and not live in a world of stories or assessments, you need to be present in the moment.

Presence is an essential state of being when you are conscious of your commitments and drive your actions towards that purpose, with a choice to create what you want. Presence is living in the moment and feeling alive to what is happening around us. Presence is seeing things that were otherwise invisible to us. Presence helps us to live the moment to its full profundity. Presence is a vital catalyst to nurturing and enhancing relations.

The bad news is your internal conversations, which are your stories, have the power to make you dance like a doll on strings. These conversations are a part of you and will never stop. The good news is you can have control over these internal conversations. Being present to these conversations is your access to altering these conversations. Once you are present to these internal conversations, you then have a choice to allow these conversations to continue or to change them.

Imagine a situation where you are stuck in a traffic jam on your way to work. You get all worked up and frustrated and hurl abuses at the situation. You can feel your eyes are rigid, your eyebrows are tensed, your stomach is squeezed in and you are taking short breaths. You are in this state for the entire 30 minutes while you are stuck at that point on the road. Your mind is busy making assessments of the impact of missing your first meeting, and being late for that all-important video call with your client.

Now imagine a situation when you are present in the moment. You are centred and you accept that there is a traffic jam and you are stuck in it. If you imagine your body in this scenario, you will realize your eyes are not tensed, your jaw is not clenched, your eyebrows are relaxed and overall you are feeling at ease and in control of the situation. In such a mind and body state, it is so much easier to think rationally and take measures to ensure your absence at work will not hamper your productivity to as large an extent.

It is human tendency to have stories going on in our heads while we see an event unfolding. Getting present to your internal conversations quickly is a matter of practice. This awareness gives you the choice of creating powerful conversations that matter to you.

Being present is very essential for dealing with breakdowns. It is being present to the assertions and also being present to the choices you have in making assessments that will impact your actions and hence results.

If presence is indeed so important, let us first begin with what does presence even mean.

To have presence is to *live* in this moment, in the *here* and *now*. Not in your past, and not in your future. To have presence is to be bodily alert in this moment. It is to be aware of your emotional state, its impact on how you see the world and also its impact on others around you.

To have presence is to be connected every moment with the question: 'for the sake of what am I doing what I am doing'. It is being connected to your purpose, and acting in fulfilling your purpose.

What I have stated earlier is the internal aspect of presence. There is another aspect to presence, which is the external aspect of presence.

Simply put, presence is how you land on other. In other words, presence is the assessment others make of your impact on them. Even before you open your mouth to speak the first word, people may make assessments about you. This assessment is based on the body you show up in and the emotional energy you emit generally, and in particular moments. Of course, once you start to speak, *what* you speak and *how* you speak also impact the way others assess your presence.

I have identified 3 Cs of presence that can significantly elevate your Leadership Presence.

First C: Choice

At IGL, we claim 'You always have a choice'. We understand that humans may have no choice in the matter of the facts of this world. For example, I have a coachee who runs a successful business, but is visually blind. In this moment, he has no choice in the matter of his eyesight, and he cannot state 'I always have choice, and I want my eyesight back'. That is not what we mean by 'You always have choice'.

My coachee may have no choice in the fact (assertion) that he is blind; however, *he always has a choice with how he approaches his blindness*. He can be disempowered about it; he can blame God for it; he can blame his destiny for it; or he can simply accept it, and move on in his life to take care of what he cares about.

In every moment, irrespective of your external circumstance, you have a choice in how you interpret your external circumstance, and how you interpret your external circumstance will determine what action you take. To be in a state of choice is also known as being centred.

We are centred when our body, mind and emotions are in a state where we can choose our actions. When we are not in a state to choose our actions, we are 'off-centre'; our reactions and tendencies choose for us.

Second C: Care

In this moment, what care are you taking care of?

Leaders are aware of their cares, and are moment-to-moment connected to what care they are taking care of. A programme participant of a 6-month programme at IGL, India, once shared:

> My team and I had created together that we, as a team, care for the vision and the goals of this organisation, and that we, as a team, would meet our goals to enable the organisation in meeting theirs. One afternoon, I returned back early to the office because my client meeting got cancelled. My entire team was sitting together and cracking jokes and generally not working. This entire team always claimed to be very busy and did not have the time to complete all the tasks they had. When I came back early, they were surprised to see me—they clearly were not expecting me back so soon to the office.
>
> I asked them, 'So, what care were you taking care of for the last hour or so in this office?'

This programme participant claimed that this simple yet powerful question opened up a new world for his team. What was blind to the team a moment ago became obvious to them a moment later.

In my interactions with my programme participants and coachees, I realize people are not even aware of what they care about. How can you take care of what you care about if you do not even know what you care for?

Third C: Commitment

Bob Dunham, the Founder of IGL, makes a claim that *our actions are shaped by our commitment*. This claim has been tested in different situations over 30 years, and not once has it been proved otherwise.

The question here is, 'Are you aware of your commitment, or are you blind to your commitment?' For example, when you go to a colleague to make a request, and the colleague responds angrily, do you clarify why you made the request you made, or do you jump to retort to his angry comment?

You had a commitment when you went up to the colleague to make a request—your action of making the request was inside of some commitment. But when you received an angry response, you lost connection with your commitment of why you were making the request in the first place, and suddenly became *committed* to teaching the other person a lesson, or defending your position, or guarding your false self-esteem, or something else of the sort.

Being connected to your commitment, moment to moment, is having presence.

Declaring breakdowns is an important leadership move; however, to be able to declare breakdowns, you need to have presence. You need to be connected with your choices, with your cares and with your commitments.

Summary and Reconstruction of Our Understanding

1. The second step after you declare a breakdown is to get clear about 'what actually happened' or 'what is so'. 'What actually happened' or 'what is so' are assertions, and are very easily confused with 'what I make of what happened' or 'what I make of what is so', which are assessments. People commonly hold their assessments as assertions, and hence, it is important to distinguish between assertions and assessments, between what is a fact and what is an opinion.

2. Here are some characteristics of assertions:

   • Assertions are claims of facts.
   • Assertions are either true or false.
   • Assertions are to a standard established by the community.
   • Assertions are speech acts that are measurable or evidentiary and can be substantiated or refuted through observation and evidence.

- Assertions reveal about the thing being observed.
- Assertions are about the past and the present.
- Assertions are where language is most descriptive and least generative.
- Assertions are not determined by moods and emotions. They are what they are, and they are not what they are not.

3. Here are some characteristics of assessments:

   - Assessments are judgements, opinions or conclusions.
   - Assessments are never true or false. However, assessments can be grounded or ungrounded.
   - Assessments can open or close possibilities for a care or a concern.
   - Assessments are a speech act and always have a speaker and a listener (the speaker and the listener can be the same person when you are having an internal conversation with yourself).
   - Assessments are also as importantly a listening act, and the reason they are called a listening act is because the way you listen to an assessment will impact what action you actually will take, and hence will impact the results you have.
   - Assessments belong to the observer, and hence reveal more about the observer than the thing being observed. Different observers make different assessments.
   - Assessments impact the future.
   - Assessments are where language is extremely generative and creative.
   - Assessments are greatly influenced by moods and emotions.

4. If the results are a function of the actions you take, and actions are a function of the assessments you make—then if you really want results, you need to question the assessments you are making.

5. Once people make an assessment, they hold on to the assessment so dearly that they find it difficult to drop an assessment that does not serve them.

6. Grounding is a practice to make assessments about assessments. Grounding does not make an assessment true; it only provides evidence and argument that it is a good assessment for our purpose. And ungrounded assessments only mean the assessments lack a relevance story with evidence to trust the assessments.

7. To ground assessments, we find answers to the following questions:

   • For the sake of what am I making this assessment?
   • In which domain of action has this assessment been made?
   • According to what or whose standard am I operating when I have made this assessment?
   • What true assertions support the assessment that I have made?
   • What true assertions are counter to the assessment that I have made?

   So in general, grounding is a way to produce more trust in an assessment.

8. What does acceptance mean?

   • Acceptance is acknowledging *what is*. Acceptance is *not* acknowledging your assessments as 'the Truth'.
   • Acceptance means that we are centred in the world *as it is* and ready for action, rather than consumed and off-centre with our *assessments or preferences about the situation*. We are ready to start from where we are.
   • We are *present*, and can take action, rather than being in our mood and conversations.
   • We are in the mood of 'it is the way it is—now what am I committed to, and what actions will I take to fulfil my commitments?' rather than the mood of 'I don't like the way it is, and I'm going to be triggered and perturbed'.
   • Acceptance has a lot to do with letting go and with letting in.

9. Presence is an essential state of being when you are conscious of your commitments and drive your actions towards that purpose, with a choice to create what you want. Presence is living in the moment and feeling alive to what is happening around us. Presence is seeing things that were otherwise invisible to us. Presence helps us to live the moment to its full profundity. Presence is a vital catalyst to nurturing and enhancing relations.

10. Following are the 3 Cs of leadership presence.

   a. choice
   b. care
   c. commitment

Generative Practices

1. Every evening give yourself 10 minutes to think about the assessments you made about the events in the day, that is, 'What are the stories you made of what was so'. Draw out a table like shown in the cases of Cedrick and Naomi. List out at least 5 events and against them write down 'what was so' and 'what did you make of what was so'.

2. Think of 3 major situations that have overwhelmed you in the past where you were totally consumed by your interpretations of the events. Remind yourself—what stories did you make that caused the overwhelm. Now think about what powerful stories you could have made in those situations and the possible difference those stories would have made to your life then.

3. In the next working day you have, bring your attention consciously to the thoughts in your mind during meetings or conversations with colleagues or even when you are busy at work. Make a mental note of them or journal them at the end of the day. You will be amazed at your findings.

4. What are the assessments you have about yourself? Get present to these assessments and ground these assessments.

5. What assessments do you have about the different people in your life?

- Spouse
- Children
- Parents
- Siblings
- Line managers (previous and current)
- Peers
- Juniors
- Friends and so forth

6. Ground these assessments using the 5-step grounding process.

7. To elevate your Leadership Presence, regularly ask yourself the following questions:

a. How am I interpreting the current situation? Is there another way to interpret this same situation?

b. For the sake of what am I doing what I am doing at this moment?

c. What am I committed to in this moment?

Reflect upon these questions. Chances are new actions will emerge for you.

8. Please journal your reflections from the above-mentioned practices. Remember, the practice of journaling is engaging in a deep conversation with yourself.

Notes

1. The term 'somatics' derives from the Greek word *somatikos*, which signifies the living, aware, bodily person. It posits that neither mind nor body is separate from the other; both being a part of a living process called the soma.

   The *soma* is often referred to as the living body in its wholeness; somatics, then is the art and science of the soma. Richard Strozzi-Heckler has provided this understanding of somatics in his book *The Art of Somatic Coaching*.

2. Bob Dunham in his Leadership papers for the Generative Leadership programme.

7
Default Future

Default future is the future that was going to happen unless something dramatic and unexpected happened. People live into the future they see coming at them, not the actual future they will get to someday. Unless people have done something radical to alter their course, the future they are living into is their default future. By default future, we do not mean the inevitable future—such as ageing and eventually dying—but rather what is going to happen in our experience, whether we give it much thought or not.[1]

Everyone has a default future. And I am not talking about the future that astrologers, palmists or numerologists talk about. This is also not the future that God has written for you, often referred to as your fate.

Like individuals, organizations, families and teams have a default future too. A default future is not a result of doing nothing, but rather the end result of current actions and plans. If this default future is not acceptable, take action that will change the trajectory to one that leads the organization to a new created future. Every relationship also has a default future.

The default future is the future that is probable, and yet almost certain. This is the future that will happen, if life continues the way it is continuing now.

The regional head for sales of a medical equipment manufacturing company mentioned to me:

I don't get along very well with a star performer in my team. I think the ways he uses to get sales may not always meet my ethical standards. He and I have disagreements on this all the time. However, at the end of the day, he helps me meet my targets and hence I choose to look the other way. However, I can now see that there is default future, a probable, almost certain future. Eventually, someone at the management will discover the ways used to sell these products, and when that happens, my relationship and credibility with the management will suffer. Also, it will further deteriorate my relationship with a star performer. All I need to do is redirect the energies of this star performer, and I will meet the targets without any of my team members doing unethical acts.

There is a default future of your relationship with your subordinates, with your seniors, with your peers, with your spouse, with your children, with your friends and with every relationship you have. Have you thought what this default future may be?

> I had a coachee who was a businessman and ran a decent-sized business. His business in the last few years was not doing very well. No new products were introduced, the market of the existing products was shrinking and generally the competition was taking over market share. In one of my early interactions with him, I asked him, 'If no new actions are taken by you, where do you see yourself 1 year, 3 years and 5 years from now?'
>
> This question is a powerful question, and it straightaway makes the connection between what we do today and the impact our today's actions have on our future.
>
> He was taken aback by this otherwise simple and obvious question. Something shifted for him in this question itself. He was evidently drifting in his professional life. He said, '1 year from now, if I don't take any major actions, my business will make further losses; and then 3 years from now, it would be exceedingly difficult to survive with the growing losses; and 5 years from now, my business would definitely be in liquidation.'
>
> This is what is meant by default future.

People can predict and foresee their default future only if they ask themselves—*what is the default future in this area?* Granted, we cannot see specific things like the date of our death or what the National Stock Exchange average will be on 31 March 2020. But we have written (*and are writing our future in the actions that we are taking and the assessments that we are making*) our own future and we do not realize it.

We all understand that if we do not save for our retirement, we are going to have to live our elderly years sparsely with nothing to get by on except depending on our children to support us or on charity. If you smoke cigarettes and continue to do so for 40 years, your default future is that you will most likely have health problems in the future.

Default Future and Its Relationship with Your Past Assessments

In one of my interactions with a group of business owners of a well-established $1 billion IT company, they stated to me that their clients were extremely demanding, did not understand the concerns of the software developers, insisted on high-quality talent working on their project, and yet were not ready to pay appropriately for their time.

By now, we know this is not *the* truth—this is *their* truth. These are not assertions; these are assessments of these business owners.

We discussed in the earlier chapter that results are a function of actions that you take and actions that you take are a function of your assessments. If the above statements are the assessments these business owners and their teams make about their clients, it is obvious how they *act* with these clients (action is driven by assessments)—like anyone would act with demanding and unreasonable people. I asked these business owners, 'What is the default future you have with these clients?' And like for the businessman coachee, I mentioned earlier, this question provoked this group to think.

They responded that eventually, some of their major customers would stop working with them. The moment they stated this, there was an immediate rejoinder stating, 'But what can we do? We are trying our best and clearly our best is not enough'.

It is interesting to note here that it is the actions of the business owners and their teams inside of their view that their customers are demanding and unreasonable that will eventually lead them to the default future. It is blind to them that their assessments of these clients are making them act the way they are acting with these clients, and that it is these actions of theirs that will lead them to this default future.

So, the point I am making here is that the default future consists of your past assessments that are now sitting in the future. These assessments make you the observer you are and now guide your actions. The actions that you take will lead you to your default future. It is like the default font appears on your screen when you type. Unless you change the settings and choose a different font, the same font will appear. If you want to change your future, change your assessments (Figure 7.1).

Assessments are powerful—they orient you to the future. Assessments determine what possibilities are open and what possibilities are closed for you. Because these are assessments, that is, *stories of which we are authors*, we now know these are not the only assessments you can make. There are other choices available. The problem we have is we tend not to associate our assessments with choices we have made. And because of this, we do not see other choices. We make our assessments–assertions, and that is pretty much what we all do. We confuse our assessments with assertions and live them as if they are true, rather than simply our interpretations. We do not take responsibility for the future we are creating with our choice of interpretations.

Figure 7.1   Assessments–Actions–Default Future

We have also discussed earlier how assessments sit in the future. If the manager gives his subordinate a target, and the subordinate assesses this target to be 'impossible', then the actions of the subordinate will be inside of this assessment of 'impossible'. These actions will lead to the result, which in this case is the subordinate's default future of not meeting the target.

The default future is largely defined by these unexamined assessments that people do not see as choices already made. In workshops, when I reveal the phenomenon of assessments that this is not *the* truth, but *your* truth, or *your* judgements, it opens up a world of new choices, and all of a sudden, the default future is not the necessary one or the only one.

And if you become aware that these are just assessments, then it becomes a particular designed set of choices that can now be changed, and we discover our generative capacity.

While a subordinate assessed the target given by his/her manager as 'impossible'—he/she did not realize that impossible was not *the truth*—it was only an assessment that he/she made. When the subordinate becomes aware that this truth is his/her creation, then he/she has the *choice* to create any other assessments (Figure 7.2).

Our assessments are embedded in the games that we play. People have lost the capacity to be the author of their games. So they get stuck in that default future because they have assessments that this is good and this is bad, that this is possible and that this is not possible. And they do not see these as assessments and thus these assessments become the rules of the game.

Figure 7.2 Awareness Gives Choice

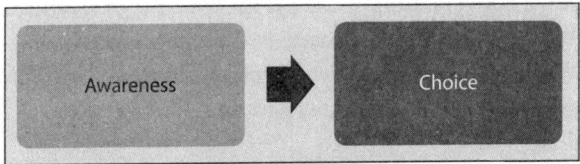

In a workshop that I conducted a few months back, a woman stated that her daughter had gained a lot of weight and that this was not healthy and she needed to lose weight. I pointed out to her that it was an assertion that her daughter had gained weight, and it was her assessment that this was not healthy and this is not how this should be.

I asked her, 'If this is the assessment you make, that this is not healthy and this is not how it should be, what action would you take?'

Her response was, 'Of course I will try to correct—I scold my daughter, I insist that she take care of her health!'

The next question I asked her, 'Does your daughter like it when you scold her? How is your relationship with your daughter?*

Her response was, 'No one likes being scolded, and neither does my daughter! This issue has certainly impacted our relationship. I don't like it that she is not taking care of her health.'

My next question to her, 'If no new action is taken, what is your default future in the matter of your relationship with your daughter?'

Like most times, this question brings out awareness to which people are blind. She realized that her default future is that her relationship with her daughter will continue to deteriorate.

The default future is most times simply a repetition of the past, or oftentimes worse.

In every area of your life, there is a default future. And the default future has a great deal to do with the assessments you are making. The question is, 'Do you know your default future? And does this default future work for you?'

We now come to the most exciting stage of declaring a breakdown. It is a stage where you create your future, or you design your future of choice.

Are you ready to declare a breakdown, assess your assessments and open a conversation of design for your future, rather than drift with the old automatic assessments you live with now?

Move on to the generative practices of this chapter, and once you have done these practices, I invite you to the next chapter of this book.

Summary and Reconstruction of Our Understanding

1. Default future is the future that is going to happen unless something dramatic and unexpected happens.
2. The default future is the future that is probable, and yet almost certain.
3. Every relationship, every area of your life, has a default future. This default future is not the same as the future that astrologers, palmists or numerologists talk about. This is also not the future that God has written for you, often referred to as your fate. Your default future in different areas of your life is a function of your actions/or inactions.
4. Like individuals, organizations, families and teams have a default future too. A default future is not a result of doing nothing, but rather the end result of current actions and plans. If your default future is not acceptable, you can take actions that will change the trajectory to one that leads you, or your family, or your team or your organization to a new created future.
5. The default future is most times simply a repetition of the past, or oftentimes worse.
6. The default future comes from your past assessments that are now sitting in the future. These assessments make you the observer you are and now guide your actions. The actions that you take will lead you to your default future.
7. Our assessments are embedded in the games that we play. People have lost the capacity to be the author of their games. So they get stuck in that default future because they have assessments that this is good and this is bad, that this is possible and that this is not possible. And they do not see these as assessments and thus these assessments become the rules of the game.
8. When you 'see' your default future, you give yourself the choice to declare a breakdown, and then to create a new future of your choice. Awareness creates choice, and hence becoming aware of the default future is critical to declaring breakdowns.

Generative Practices

I invite you to consider and journal your default future in the following areas:

1. *Health:* Your body, diet, health, sleep, daily routine and so on.
2. *Family:* Your relationship with your spouse, children, parents, siblings, friends and so on.
3. *Career and organization:* This includes your and your family's financial security, career satisfaction, taking care of the interest of your clients, juniors, seniors, peers and so on.
4. *Hobbies:* Your passions and your creative life.
5. *Emotional:* Your deepest positive emotions and your darkest fears.
6. And any other area in which you would like to distinguish your default future.

To help you become aware of your default future, here are some questions for you to ask yourself in each area of your life:

1. *If no new action is taken, what is likely to happen in this area of your life in the foreseeable future?*
   This is an important conversation about your default future. This future is probable and almost certain, and yet you are choosing to remain ignorant about this future. I recommend that you make a note of your response to this question. Write down all the good, the not so good and the bad.
2. *If this was the future, what would be the automatic actions you would be taking, such that this future would really happen?*
   Please make a note of these too. Up until now, you have been taking these actions blindly, and these actions are leading you to your default future.
3. *Finally, ask yourself the question, 'Does this default future work for me?'*

If the answer is 'yes', then continue taking the actions that you will be taking (the ones that you have made a note of in the earlier point). However, if the answer is 'no', this default future does not work for you, then read on. In the next chapter, we will talk about creating a new future.

Every action and decision we make today impacts our goals, colleagues, team, organization, family and friends. While you are considering the above questions, I also want you to imagine how your actions impact the default future of people around you.

(Please do not worry if your default future gets you concerned. As a matter of fact, for some of you, chances are it may. I would like you to be aware of your default future, which may be blind to you currently. This awareness will present a choice to create a new future, which is the topic of the next chapter.)

Note

1. Steve Zaffron and Dave Logan, *The Three Laws of Performance: Rewriting the Future of Your Organization and Your Life* (California: Jossey-Bass/Wiley/ Times Group Books, 2009).

8

Creating a New Future

Default Future Versus Created Future

We have already discussed the default future in an earlier chapter. In each area of your care, you already have a default future, that is, a future that is probable and almost certain. And, you do not know that you do not know (*not knowing that you do not know is blindness*) this is your default future, which is normally blind to us.

Why? Because you have never asked yourself the question, 'What is my default future in this particular area of my life?' Chances are, your default future is simply a repetition of the past, or sometimes even worse.

Every action you take, inside of your assessment, leads you to some result or another. Unfortunately, while some people manage their actions effectively, very few question the assessments that drive them to act. We have also already looked at how these assessments drive you to your default future.

If you have not asked yourself 'What is my default future in a particular area of my life?', chances are that you will be surprised when you get to that future. And you may find people and circumstances to blame for your default future.

If you are lucky, your environment will change or the people around you will change, and you may have a different future than your default future. However, this will have nothing to do with you.

This book is an invitation to you to create your future, powerfully, with choice.

Conversations for Possibilities

People are involved in conversations for possibilities all the time. Yet, they are not aware that they are engaged in these conversations, and these conversations are happening loosely without understanding the impact of these conversations.

Let me share an example from the late 1990s. I ran an education company (franchising company) that franchised some of its programmes. We had a franchisee company, in one of the major cities of India that once stated to me 'the targets you have set are impossible'.

In effect, what the franchisee company was stating (not explicitly, but implicitly) was 'I declare that the targets you have set are not possible, and that my actions will not result in achieving these targets'. The franchisee company did not even realize that they were engaged in a conversation for possibility, and that they declared in this conversation the context for their actions. Once you make a declaration, your actions, consciously or subconsciously, are then based on this declaration that you make.

For 3 years, my company worked with this franchisee company, and in each year, the franchisee fell way below their targets.

Eventually, my company terminated the contract and invited another company to take on the franchise. By now, to a certain extent, we had started to believe that our targets were too high. This new franchisee, on being given the targets, stated, 'Is that all your targets are? That is easy. What are the bonuses for exceeding the targets?' This new franchisee company declared 'that is easy', and their actions were taken inside of this declaration. They were also engaged in a *conversation for possibility*. And chances are, even they did not know this.

The targets were the same for the old and the new franchisees. The new franchisee over exceeded the targets in the first 6 months.

Conversations for possibilities are pervasive and we are all engaged in them. Some conversations for possibilities close possibilities and others open possibilities.

The first franchisee 'created' a future around the assessment that 'this target was impossible'. They closed possibilities with this creation. The actions that these people took subconsciously fell inside of the context that 'the target was not possible'.

The second franchisee 'created' a future, suggesting 'these were easy targets and that they could exceed these targets'. They opened up possibilities with this creation. The actions these people took were inside of a context, suggesting that the targets were low and that they wanted to earn the bonus for exceeding the target.

What you speak opens and closes possibilities.

What Does Possibility Mean?

The use of the word 'possibility' in this case is not about possibilities being something that may or may not be possible—a phenomenon of luck or destiny. For example, it is possible for the Kenyan cricket team to beat the Australian cricket team, yet it is improbable or unlikely based on the way Kenyan cricket is currently set up.

The common-sense understanding of possibility, as per the *Oxford Dictionaries*, is 'a thing that may happen'.[1] I am also not talking about this possibility that may happen someday in the future.

The possibility that I am talking about here is a creation of your doing that empowers you in this moment and shapes the way you think and feel about taking new action. When you create this kind of a possibility, you impact your 'now'. You impact your present.

For example, in my declaration, when I created the possibility of setting up IGL in India, it changed the way I felt in that moment. I felt a new surge of energy, a new power to take actions that were hitherto unknown to me.

When you create a new possibility, it excites you automatically and puts you in the mood for taking action right now. You know you can make the possibility a reality, as long as you take actions in line with achieving this possibility.

Let us take the same example of the Kenyan cricket team beating the Australian cricket team. Cricket Kenya (the association that manages and runs cricket in Kenya) may create the possibility of beating Australia in cricket consistently. And once they create this as a possibility, they need to back this with actions inside of making this possibility come alive. If this is a possibility that excites the team management and players of Cricket Kenya, then they will become energized and take new actions, actions which they did not take earlier and which were as a matter of fact blind to them.

When a family gets together and discusses a family vacation, they are engaged in a conversation for possibility.

When the board members of an organization get together and discuss opening a new branch, introducing a new product, adding a new feature—they are engaged in a conversation for possibility.

When members of a team discuss new goals for the following financial year, they are engaged in a conversation for possibility.

Create a Future of Your Choice

My coach Bob Dunham often states, 'Create a future of your choice; because you are creating your future anyway'. Whether you agree with gravity or not, whether you like it or not, it has an impact in your life. Similarly, whether we know it or not, accept it or reject it, each one of us is engaged in a constant process of creating our future.

As discussed earlier, you are engaged in a conversation for possibility anyway—these conversations shape the way you see the future, and the actions that you take today. A manager who is committed to building a future for his/her organization can engage others in conversations for possibilities to generate a new future. Once a new future has been created in a conversation, the organization and the people around start to show up differently. You begin to 'see' *new* openings, *new* opportunities and *new* avenues for action.

There is a claim that I would like to make here, and the claim is 'you are alive because you create'. Aliveness is different from breathing and existing. Brother David Steindl-Rast[2] states, 'the fact that you are not yet dead is not sufficient proof that you are alive'. Aliveness is creating a future that brings you 'alive', that has you energized, purposeful, engaged and fulfilled in your actions and experiences.

L. Ron Hubbard defines livingness as 'livingness is going along a certain course impelled by a purpose and with some place to arrive. It consists mostly of removing the barriers in the channel, holding the edges firm, ignoring the distractions and reinforcing and re-impelling one's progress along the channel. That's Life'.[3]

This 'purpose' or the 'place to arrive' that L. Ron Hubbard is talking about in his definition of livingness is the future that you create. Case in point is The 5 AM Club I referred to earlier in this book. Each one of us, members of The 5 AM Club, created a future of our choice, and received support from the other members in 'removing barriers in the channel', 'holding the edges firm', 'ignoring the distractions' and 'continuing to progress along the channel'.

You Are Always Only One Conversation Away from Creating a New Future

I have run into people and coached people who could not speculate. They could absolutely not create a new future, given their history, that is, the assessments within which they had led their life. And on my invitation, when they did create a new future, they actually became afraid. These were people who were so used to living a life of drift, a life of no choice—that when an opportunity to create with choice emerged, it took them into an unknown zone. They wanted to exit this zone quickly and get back into the zone of comfort—a zone of no choice!

The key is to see the power you have to create; once you do this, most of the battle is won. Most people simply do not believe they have this power to create and have not lived life from this disclosive space. Irrespective of the way you have lived your life—you are always only one conversation away from creating a new future.

One of my favourite quotations is from *The Four Agreements* by Don Miguel Ruiz.[4] He states:

> Your word is the power that you have to create. Through the word you express your creative power. It is through the word that you manifest everything. Regardless of what language you speak, your intent manifests through the word. The word is not just a written sound or a symbol. The word is a force; it is the power you have to create the events in your life.

It is a practice to develop, to be present or alive to the future you are creating. When you get it (when I use the phrase 'get it', I do not mean you understand what I am saying. I mean you get it in your body, after having experienced it. You have embodied it), you realize that you are creating your future anyway and feel this in all parts of your being: mind, body and soul.

And if you are creating your future anyway, you might as well create a future of choice. Right now, in this moment, you can have a new conversation and create a new future for yourself—in any area of your life. Because you are always only one conversation away from creating a new future.

The Challenge of Creating a New Future Without Knowing How to Achieve It

Some people get paralysed by the thought of creating a new future if they do not know how to achieve this future.[5] The general common sense of our way of life is 'I need to know how first' and then I will be able to declare 'what future I can create'. This is a misunderstanding of our common culture. My claim is the 'what' needs to come first, and then the 'how'.

People in our culture have been educated and trained to know things, to develop reliable skills and to act out of their familiarity and competence. And so we keep our work and actions in the zones with which we have become familiar and competent.

Yet we see some people who seem to have skills at the edge. They do not withdraw from the unknown. They actually see the unknown as possibilities, and may even love the unknown. They move skilfully in the unknown—they are curious. They explore, analyse, speculate, design, invent, innovate and plan. They show up as leaders, entrepreneurs, innovators and explorers.

For most people in our culture, 'not knowing' stops them—they must know to act. In generative leadership, 'not knowing' is a place to begin action. Here our first action is to 'know', and then to invent a new value.

Taking action with 'not knowing' is a skill, and one that is fundamental to leadership. And skills are developed through consistent practice. We must be able to notice the fear and contraction that 'I don't know' can produce, and learn to make fear our friend. Bert Bennett, my coach Bob Dunham's friend and teacher, says, 'fear is just your body telling you that you are not organized for the situation'.

If we can go from *being* afraid, to *having* fear, then we can observe and engage with the fear from a place of choice. Awareness creates choice. If we develop this awareness, then we can develop essential skills at the edge for us as leaders, professionals and human beings. By becoming aware of our body reactions and emotions, we open the path to learning how to engage with them and to shift them.

When we manage our reactions at the edge, we can hold the unknown as a sea of possibilities for what we care about. We can embody the skills of creating from the unknown with practices of exploration, experimentation, design, invention and innovation.

We all have experienced the unknown with learning in our careers. When we took on a new job requiring new skills or responsibilities, we may have found the learning challenging, difficult or exhilarating. As we developed competence, we became more comfortable in our knowledge and skill.

(All the members of The 5 AM Club created new futures and each one of us did not know 'how' we would achieve these new futures that we created. The 'what' came before the 'how'. Please refer to the preface for these examples.)

Summary and Reconstruction of Our Understanding

1. People are involved in conversations for possibilities all the time. Yet, they are not aware that they are engaged in these conversations, and these conversations are happening loosely without people understanding the impact of these conversations.

2. Some conversations for possibilities close possibilities and others open possibilities.

3. In language, you create possibilities, that which did not exist till you created them in language. When you create such a possibility, it empowers you in this moment and shapes the way you think and feel about taking new action. When you create this kind of a possibility, you impact your 'now'. You impact your present.

4. When you create a new possibility, it excites you automatically and puts you in the mood for taking action right now. You know you can make the possibility a reality, as long as you take actions in line with achieving this possibility.

5. Whether you agree with gravity or not, whether you like it or not, it has an impact in your life. Similarly, whether we know it or not, accept it or reject it, each one of us is engaged in a constant process of creating our future.

6. *You are most alive when you are creating.* Aliveness is different from breathing and existing.

7. The key is to see the power you have to create; once you do this, most of the battle is won. Most people simply do not believe they have this power to create and have not lived life from this disclosive space. Irrespective of the way you have lived your life—you are always only one conversation away from creating a new future.

8. It is a practice to develop, to be present or alive to the future you are creating.

9. The general common sense of our way of life is 'I need to know how I will achieve' first and then I will be able to declare 'what future I can create'. This is a misunderstanding of our common culture. My claim is the 'what' needs to come first, and then the 'how' starts to get disclosed.

10. For most people in our culture, 'not knowing' stops them—they must know to act. In generative leadership, 'not knowing' is a place to begin action. Here our first action is to 'know', and then to invent new value.

11. Taking action with 'not knowing' is a skill, and one that is fundamental to leadership.

12. Creating a new future is critical to declaring a breakdown. When you declare a breakdown, you are in effect stating that the default future is not OK with you, and that you are at the source of creating a future of your choice.

Generative Practices

You reflected upon your default future in different areas of your life in the previous chapter. If your default future does not work for you in any area of your life, this practice is an invitation for you to design a new future of choice in those areas of your life.

1. *Health:* Your body, diet, health, sleep, daily routine and so on.

2. *Family:* your relationship with your spouse, children, parents, siblings, friends and so on.

3. *Career and organization:* This includes your and your family's financial security, career satisfaction, taking care of the interest of your clients, juniors, seniors, peers and so on.

4. *Hobbies:* Your passions and your creative life.
5. *And any other area* in which you would like to design a new future.

Please create a new future in the above-mentioned areas, or where required.

Once you have designed or created your new future, the next step is to take actions to achieve the future. Please read on to the next chapter of Missing Actions.

Please journal the declarations of your new future. Please also be present, and mindful of what is arising for you from these questions. For example, fear of declaring a future, or questions such as how will you achieve this future, or there is no point in doing this exercise—this is yet another one of those activities that really do not give results, and so on. Be aware of these assessments—understand that these are assessments and not assertions. Give yourself a choice if you would like to continue with these assessments.

Creating a future is not only about creating a long-term future. Every time there is an interruption in your life, you have a choice to declare a breakdown and create a new future. On an ongoing basis, use interruptions in your life as opportunities to create a future of your choice.

Notes

1. http://www.oxforddictionaries.com/definition/english/possibility?q=Possibility&searchDictCode=all, accessed 16 February 2016.
2. David Steindl-Rast, *Gratefulness, the Heart of Prayer: An Approach to Life in Fullness* (Mahwah, NJ: Paulist Press, 1984). http://www.gratefulness.org/readings/dd_abcs_h-j.htm
3. L. Ron Hubbard, *Dianetics and Scientology Technical Dictionary* (Denmark: New Era Publications, 1975, 1978).
4. Don Miguel Ruiz, *The Four Agreements* (California: Amber-Allen Publishing, Inc., 1997, 2012).
5. Bob Dunham has a yet unpublished paper called the 'Power of Not Knowing'. I came across this paper in my education at IGL, USA, and found this concept powerful. I have referred to the above-mentioned paper in this section.

9
Identifying Missing Actions

In the Introduction chapter of the book, I spoke about the centrality of conversations. Fernando Flores talks about his understanding of language being the fundamental characteristic that makes us human. He adds, 'but language also has the dimension of acts—the way we do things with language, and that language does with us'.[1]

Further, he states, 'I gained conviction that there is a whole other world that is just as important, and no less rational—a world that is emotional, social, and historical. This is the world in which, in collaboration with others, we bring forth realities, negotiate with each other, and make history happen, all in conversations with each other'.

When you declare a breakdown, and reach the step of 'identifying missing actions'—I invite you to be the observer who will look for the missing language acts that we distinguish in this chapter.

What Does 'Action' Mean?

Bob Dunham, the Founder of IGL, defines our cultural common sense of action as 'acts that shape subsequent movement'. Further, he points out that the whole frame of speech and listening acts are future creating acts.

The common-sense understanding of language is that action is movement. However, the claim we make at IGL is that all action is shaped by language, and the generative acts of language are the actions that shape subsequent actions (which I call 'execution' in this book).

So, in effect, action equals generative acts in language, and also, physical action that is shaped because of these generative language acts.

Let us look at the anatomy of action,[2] as developed by Bob Dunham, the Founder of IGL, USA.

Anatomy of Action

Here are some fundamental claims (Figure 9.1):

1. *Outcomes or results are a function of actions.*
   You can use any number of different words, but the key point is—*it is actions that give you results.* Results are a function of your actions. You take action and you get results, based on the action you take. You do not take actions and you do not have results. Some may argue that 'no result' is also a kind of a result. I agree. In that case, 'no action' is also

Figure 9.1   Anatomy of Action

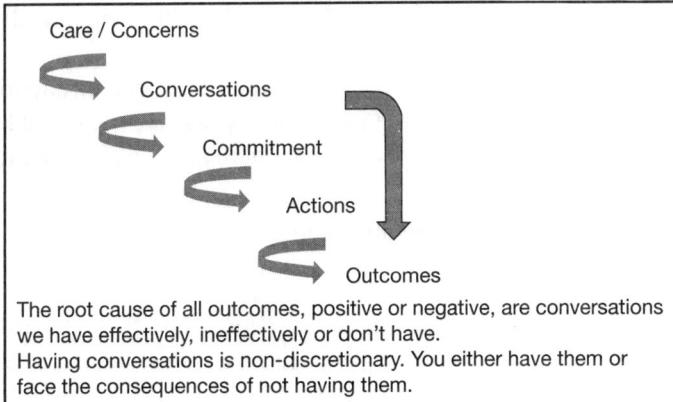

Care / Concerns

Conversations

Commitment

Actions

Outcomes

The root cause of all outcomes, positive or negative, are conversations we have effectively, ineffectively or don't have.
Having conversations is non-discretionary. You either have them or face the consequences of not having them.

Source: © Bob Dunham. All rights reserved internationally.

some kind of action. So, action of 'no action' will give you a result of 'no result' or a result that may not be satisfactory or acceptable. For example, Peter is speeding and he knows this but takes no action to slow down. The police stop him and the result is he gets a ticket. Similarly, Allen sits all day in front of his TV and watches sports channels. The result is his family does not have food on the table. His 'inaction' of not working to earn money, and his 'action' of watching sports channels all day, gives him the result of no food on the table.

We also 'decide' that no intervention or action will produce what we want, so we take the action of abiding with what is happening anyway. It is an active choice. The problem is that we often do not see it as a choice being made by us, and we give up our power to choose in the story and emotion of resignation.

For example, assessments we make such as 'I cannot make a difference', or 'I cannot go against authority', or 'I am not good enough to act' are stories that create a mood of resignation and give us our choice of no action.

In a health care services company where I delivered a keynote talk, the vice-president stated to me, 'The powers are not with me. The Board takes all the decisions, and tells us what to do, so what's the point of me doing anything—it will be rejected by the board in any case.' The vice-president was blind to the 'choice' he was making. He was making an assessment (he was blind to the choice he had in making this assessment—he thought this assessment was 'the truth'), and that assessment was giving him the emotion of resignation. Because of that assessment and the emotion of resignation, he continued to take no action.

In our life, we are constantly looking for how to improve our actions, to improve our results. For that to happen, the interpretation that action is movement and activity does not help. We need to use the interpretation that action is *generative acts in language that shape subsequent action*.

One fundamental 'generative act' that creates and shapes our movement and behaviour is commitment.

2. *Action is shaped by commitment.*

As pointed out in the Introduction chapter, John Austin, the philosopher of language, shows us that we perform *acts* in language that are not descriptive, but that generate commitments and the future. He discovered that when we make a promise, for example, we are not describing something in the world. Instead, we are making an act, and the act is one of commitment—showing what the speaker is committed to—for the future.

John commits to Raj that he will complete compiling the text for their organization's promotional material by 30 November. This act of commitment then shapes the physical action that John takes of compiling the text for the promotional material. Without the commitment, that action of compiling the text would not take place.

Another example is that of Peter and his morning jog. Peter set the alarm for 5.30 AM to go for his morning jog. When the alarm rang, Peter promptly woke up and put the alarm off. After putting the alarm off, Peter looked outside the window. It was dark and cold. He started to question whether he was better off going for the jog, or taking another 30 minutes more to sleep. He decided to sleep for 30 more minutes.

In that moment, the 'action' taken by Peter of going back to sleep was inside his commitment to comfort, rather than his commitment to his health.

Our actions are shaped by commitment—the commitments we make or do not make, commitments we know or we do not even know, the clarity of our commitment and the ownership and importance of the commitment to the person or organization committing.

3. *Commitments arise in conversations.*

Where do commitments come from? They always arise in conversations. Even commitments with ourselves arise in conversation, or can be traced back to an earlier conversation. Commitment is what shapes and drives action. In the earlier examples, John committed to Raj, in conversation, that he would complete compiling the text for their organization's promotional material and Peter, in conversation with himself, chose to go back to sleep, rather than step out for a jog.

If you want to change your commitments, change your conversations. If you want new commitments, have new conversations. If you want others to make new commitments, have new conversations with them (we will discuss this in detail in the next chapter 'Conversation for Action').

4. *Our care determines what commitments have meaning for us.*
   Care is fundamental to being human. Human beings are beings of care.

   We can bring our care and concerns to our conversations, or have our conversations only be degraded discussions of transactions and activities. To take care of the cares we have, we need to have commitments inside of each of our cares. When our commitments are inside of our care, that is when our commitments have meaning.

   Action in which we care about the performance and result is very different than when we do not care. A multi-year research project done by McKinsey & Company, whose results they have described in their recent book *The Progress Principle*, found that of all the events that can deeply engage people in their jobs, the single most important one is making progress in meaningful work.[3] Our claim is exactly that; our care determines what commitments have meaning for us.

5. *All results, both individually and socially, have as their root cause in* prior conversations, *conversations that are had, conversations that are missing, conversations that are performed well or poorly.*[4]
   Conversations are not just language, but interactions that involve and are shaped by the body and emotions as well, and have a background of history and practice. The anatomy of action is not just a model. The relationships described in the anatomy of action are not discretionary. They exist in reality if we have the eyes to see them, and we pay the

penalty of blindness if we ignore them. This perspective gives us a generative place to look for how to generate, shape, influence and produce the outcomes and results that others and we value.

6. *Conversations always include the coherence of SELPH, that is, Somatic, Emotion, Language, Practice and History.*

In Chapter 2, Centrality of Conversations, we looked at a new way of understanding conversations. Our claim at IGL is that your conversations are a coherence of SELPH, that is, Somatic, Emotion, Language, Practice and History, and it is conversations that are the root cause of all outcomes. Having conversations is non-discretionary. You either have them or face the consequences of not having them. Please refer to the reconstructed definition of 'conversation' in Chapter 2. All elements of SELPH are included in that definition of conversation.

Missing Conversations

Talk is powerful. You need to engage in the right conversation at the right time. This is crucial for your personal and organizational success. To look for the missing conversation is not a part of our cultural reality. However, the claim that I make here is:

If you do not have the results that you want, there are missing conversations that you need to distinguish first and then have—with others and with yourself. If you have different conversations, you can have different results. And if you want different results, you must have different conversations.

Ask yourself a simple question: 'What can be a missing conversation in this case?' In doing so, you set your mind thinking in the direction to look for a missing conversation, rather than stating 'this is not possible', 'this simply cannot be done' and so forth.

If you 'listen' for dissatisfaction in and around your organization, you will begin to distinguish the missing or broken conversations. With practice, you will not only see the conversations that shape the organization and its actions and results but also begin to have the sensibility to see the missing conversations. For example, dissatisfaction in a certain area is a symptom of a missing promise in that area; if it were fulfilled, it would produce satisfaction instead of dissatisfaction. This missing promise may be the result of a missing request. The missing request may be the result that people are not clear who is responsible or authorized to make such requests.

By understanding what the conversations would look like to produce a desired result, we can see the missing conversations in the current situation. This may be an opportunity to declare a breakdown.

Once you have declared the breakdown, and created a new future, a powerful question is, 'What conversations are missing that would produce this new created future?' The reason this is a powerful question is because once you have asked this question, you 'listen' for missing conversations.

Let us now look at listening as unavoidable, crucial and powerful action.

The Listening Act

We have spoken about the importance of conversations. What we have not spent much time discussing is 'listening'. Listening is an interpretation that the listener makes based on his or her context. The listening context of every individual is different, and hence, while the speaker says this one thing, and if there are five listeners, each of the five listeners listen differently based on their individual contexts and backgrounds.

The listening context of an individual is determined by his/her disclosive space, that is, history, culture, practices, past assessments, body and moods and emotions (we discussed the disclosive space in Chapter 4).

Listening is a fundamental capacity of leadership. It is the background structure of interpretation that gives meaning to whatever we perceive. So, when two people are in a conversation, there are actually three conversations going on, and are as follows:

- First is the conversation between the two people
- Second is the conversation one person has internally with himself/herself
- Third is the conversation the other person has internally with himself/herself

Building your leadership capacity is to choose what internal conversation you have with yourself (what assessments you make), because this internal conversation you have with yourself determines what conversation you have with the external person. And the key focus is also on what listening you are producing in the other person.

This internal conversation that you have with yourself is the assessments (story) that you make up, and as discussed, assessments drive your actions and actions drive your results.

Assessments live in the present and shape future. Once you make an assessment, then you 'listen' for that assessment. In an earlier chapter, I gave an example of my coachee, Tanvir, who assessed himself to be shy. Once he made that assessment, he 'listened' to himself as shy, that is, he continued to look for evidence that he is shy. If he looked for evidence that he was shy—guess what he found! He obviously found evidence that he is shy. When I asked him to look for evidence of his boldness to reach the position of a senior director in a global software development firm, he found that. He realized that he *was not* shy, but he had continued to listen for his shyness and hence he only found that.

A new claim: You get what you 'listen' for.

There are different types of listening. We will look at the 4 important types of listening in this book, each of which has relevance in the conversation of missing actions to achieve the new created future (Figure 9.2).

1. Listening to make yourself right/to make the other wrong
2. Listening for objective facts
3. Listening for care and commitment
4. Listening for possibilities

Figure 9.2 Four Important Types of Listening

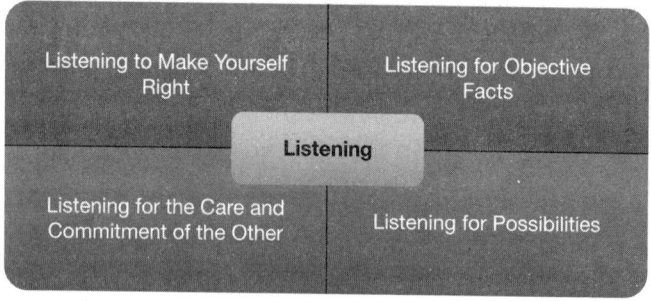

Listening to Make Yourself Right

This is the kind of listening that Tanvir was involved in. Once Tanvir made an assessment that *he is shy*, he continued to listen to make himself right by listening for evidence of his shyness. This is the default listening of people.

As humans, we are assessment-making machines, and we do not even realize that we make assessments, hold these to be the truth, forget we made this up and then listen for evidence to continuously and subconsciously validate this truth. When you powerfully create a new future through your declarations, you tune your mind to listen to see how you can make this future come alive.

Listening for Objective Facts

Leaders consciously look for objective facts, and do not always depend on their past assessments. Leaders look for assertions (objective facts) and then make grounded assessments. They do not depend on their past ungrounded assessments. I had a coachee who was a partner in an international accounting company, who in his first or second session itself made a casual remark by stating that 'women are not good drivers'. I asked him if this was an assertion or an assessment, and he cheekily said, 'Yes, this is an assessment, yet a grounded one'. I said, 'OK, why don't we do this? Before our next session which is scheduled for next week, while driving, look for good women drivers, and tell me what you find'.

The next week when we met, I asked him what he found. He said, 'You were right, Sameer. I found a lot of good women drivers. I did see a few not so good women drivers, but then I also found a few not so good men drivers!' The difference between his listening was that earlier he was subconsciously listening to make himself right (women are not good drivers), and the next one week, he chose to listen for objective facts.

Once you have created the new future, you want to engage in listening for objective facts, so that you can use these facts to make new assessments to generate new actions and results.

Listening for Care and Commitment

Earlier in this chapter, we looked at the anatomy of action. We saw that action comes from commitment, and commitment comes from care. You can choose to listen for care and commitment of the other. A senior project manager with an IT company was having trouble with one of her subordinates. She thought this subordinate was a good worker, but arrogant and not a team player; he did not follow instructions and wanted to do his own thing. Every time she tried having a conversation with him, the conversation would end up in an argument.

The senior project manager tried to speak in different ways, sometimes softly and calmly, and sometimes with authority—but nothing worked for her. And the reason for nothing working for her in any of the conversations was because she continued to listen to make herself right (*by listening for this subordinate being arrogant and not a team player*). She did not realize that she was continuing to listen for her past assessments of this subordinate, and irrespective of how she spoke, she found evidence of the assessments she had made.

In a workshop, I asked her, 'What do you think is the care and the commitment of this person?' Interestingly, this question directed her attention to something that she had never listened for in this subordinate. It was a moment of shift for this young lady. She said in the workshop, 'Oh my God, I never thought of this!' A few weeks later, in a follow-up session, she shared that her relationship with her subordinate was transformed and all it took was for her to listen for his care and commitment.

Leadership is about creating a shared future with others. This can only happen when we create shared care, and shared commitments. This is why we must listen for care and commitment, and invite others to conversations where we co-create shared cares and commitments in conversations.

Listening for Possibilities

My claim is there are possibilities all around us, except most of us have not developed the eyes to see these possibilities and the ears to listen for these possibilities. Every relationship is a possibility; every conversation is a possibility; every moment offers a possibility. Humans are so engrossed in listening to make themselves right, they are losing out on listening for possibilities. Think of a leader that you admire, and chances are you will see the difference between this leader, and others, is that this leader continued to/ continues to look for possibilities. If this leader looked for possibilities, guess what he finds/found.

Possibilities!

The leader you admire acts/acted on the possibilities that she/ he sees/saw and hence achieves/achieved the results that make/ made her/him the leader that you admire.

People wait for the right opportunity to come by. Right opportunities do not come by. You need to 'listen' for the right opportunities. *They are all around.* You need to develop the eyes to 'see' these opportunities; you need to develop the ears to 'listen' to these opportunities.

Leaders begin with conversations.

In conversations, they begin by first 'listening'. It is a myth that you begin conversations by speaking. You begin conversations by first choosing what you want to listen for.

And you listen for

- objective facts,
- care and commitment and
- possibilities.

Reflective Pause

Take a moment to pause and observe what it is that you are generally listening for.

Recognize that you have a choice in this matter. Remember, what you 'see' is a function of what you listen for.

Different Types of Conversations

Once we have declared a breakdown, assessed the default future and created a new future, we now have to take actions to achieve this new future. Earlier in this chapter, we reconstructed the meaning of the word 'action' stating that all action is shaped by language (conversations), and the generative acts of language are itself actions that shape subsequent actions.

If action is conversation, and if these generative conversations shape subsequent action, then we need to look at the different types of important conversations.

There are several different types of conversations that you have with others. I am listing the important ones in the context of declaring breakdowns (Figure 9.3).

- Conversation for relationships
- Conversation for possibilities
- Conversation for action

The conversation for action happens inside of the context of the conversation for possibilities, and the conversation for possibilities happens inside of the context of conversation for relationships.

Figure 9.3   Important Types of Conversations

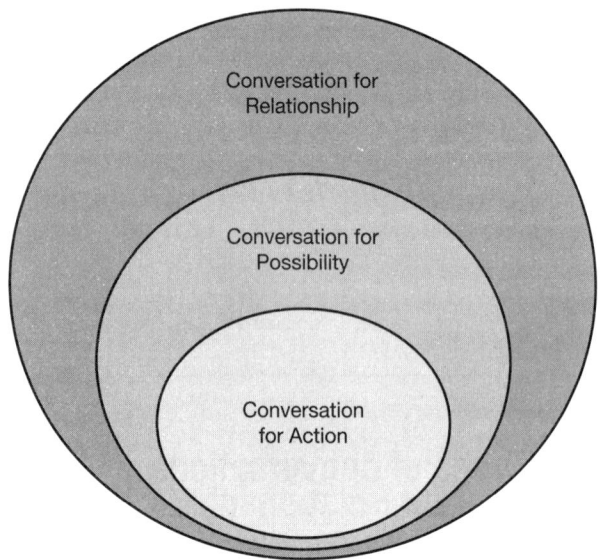

In each of these conversations, here is what you listen for (Figure 9.4):

Conversation for relationship

- Shared interest
- Shared care
- Shared commitment

Conversation for possibilities

- Emerging possibilities

Conversation for action

- Conditions of satisfaction
- Commitment
- Care (for the sake of what?)

Figure 9.4 What Do You Listen for in Different Conversations?

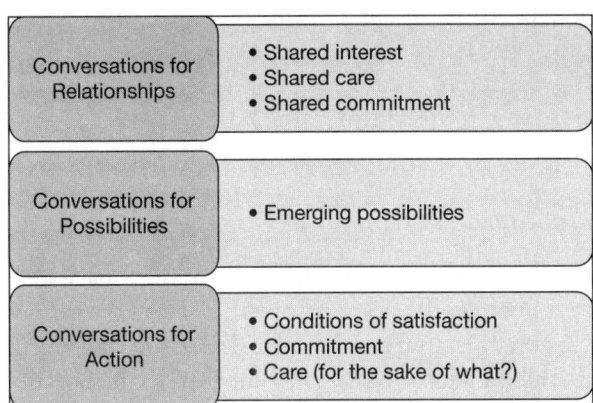

Conversations for Relationships	• Shared interest • Shared care • Shared commitment
Conversations for Possibilities	• Emerging possibilities
Conversations for Action	• Conditions of satisfaction • Commitment • Care (for the sake of what?)

Conversation for Relationship

To get meaningful and productive results with other people, the first conversation you need to have is a *conversation for relationship*.

Conversations for relationship create a foundation of workability in which people are free to express their concerns and make open requests. Participants in this conversation relate to each other as a function of their commitments, instead of relating to each other based on the assessments, interpretations and feelings they have about each other. Rather than resigning themselves to patterns of defensive behaviour, resentment or cynicism, they focus on building relationships and opening possibilities through their speaking and listening.

The objective of this conversation is to discover the basis for collaboration between individuals. What I mean by this is to establish, at a very minimum, some sense of *shared interest* between individuals from which action can arise. What can be a deeper and more powerful basis for a relationship is a *shared concern* or a shared care about some issue or topic. For a conversation for relationships to get most effective, you need to discover a *shared commitment* among individuals in the conversation (Figure 9.5).

Figure 9.5   Element of a Conversation for Relationship

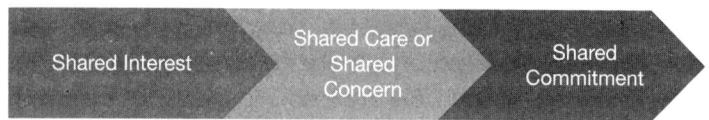

For example:

Shared interest: Two individual organizations have a shared interest in organ donation. While this is useful to know that another organization has the same shared interest, it provides a basis, albeit a loose basis, for some future collaboration.

Shared care or concern: While these organizations are interested in organ donation, finding out that both these organizations are concerned, in particular, about the dismal organ donation numbers in India provides for a more focused set of possibilities.

Shared commitment: But it is only when these organizations declare a shared commitment, such as a desire to run a focused education programme for transplant coordinators in hospitals next year, that they immediately open clear possibilities for focused coordinated action.

And all of this can only be accomplished by taking the time to talk, having conversations.

Conversations for relationship require us to slow down, to do our best to understand one another, to suspend judgement, to be curious and to listen—deeply. We allow our own world to be touched and opened, by the world of other people. Done well, we give our aspirations wings through the trust of others and the shared sense of being up to something that matters.

Perhaps you can immediately see the difficulties that arise if we dive into action without having this conversation. Yet it happens all the time. We declare ourselves 'a team' and think we will accomplish our team goals, when we have not even figured out whether we care about anything in common. And then we wonder why our experience of working together feels so lifeless and confusing. Or, because we cannot tolerate or talk about our feelings of anxiety and urgency, we start to do things before we even know why we are doing them, with all too predictable consequences.

In the world of organizations at the moment in time, the pressure to move quickly away from conversations for relationship seems to be growing. It is like leaving out the foundation because you are in a hurry to get the house up.

We all know how that turns out.

In Chapter 5, in 'Team Breakdowns' section, I spoke about the Houston, Texas, based IT company, where I did a 6-month programme. One of the first things the participants of the programme, who were all managers, did was to have effective conversations for relationships among themselves first, and then with each of their subordinates. There was complete alignment in their interest and care for the organization and, most importantly, complete alignment in their commitments to a new result that they, as a team, wanted to generate. As we noted earlier, this team, within 4 months itself, achieved the result they committed to.

Conversations for relationships are integral conversations, and most times are the missing conversations, that managers and executives in the corporate world do not regularly have.

In my assessment, conversations for relationships are integral conversations for parents, for couples and also for friends to have. An alignment in your cares and commitments is key to having a satisfying relationship.

Conversation for Relationship

Conversations for Relationship create a foundation of workability in which people are free to express their concerns and make open requests.

What do you listen for in this conversation?
Participants listen for the care and commitment of the other. What you consciously do not listen for is your past assessments, interpretations and feelings for each other—if these are disempowering.

Focus is on
The focus in this type of conversation is to build relationships and open possibilities through speaking and listening.

Objective of the conversation
The objective of this conversation is to discover:

- Shared Interest
- Shared Care and Concern
- Shared Commitment

Reflective Pause

In which of your relationships is a conversation for relationship missing currently? With your subordinates, peers, seniors, family, friends and so forth?

How will having this conversation impact the result you have in your relationship with these people?

Conversation for Possibility

A missing conversation may even be a conversation for possibility. A conversation for possibility generates ideas for possible action. Once you have identified your cares, and in conversations for relationships, distinguished shared cares with your colleagues, team members, clients, family and so on—you engage in a conversation for possibility.

This conversation is conducted in a mood of curiosity and speculation, identifying possible future actions without judging them or committing to them. Its purpose is to generate a range of possible outcomes, especially including many that are not obvious in habitual frameworks and within current constraints. To maintain the mood of speculation and generate the richest set of possibilities, the speakers must wilfully refrain from making feasibility assessments and commitment. An example is a 'what if' conversation requested by a team member to explore a proposal. Another example is a group brainstorming session that designs goals or ways around obstacles.

We briefly touched upon conversation for possibility in the previous chapter. The structure for conversations for possibilities includes the following elements (Figure 9.6):

1. Listen
2. Speculate
3. Choose
4. Declare

Listening for Possibilities

The first step of this conversation is to listen for possibilities. I hear people talking in language such as 'this is not possible'. It is important to understand that possibilities do not exist as real

Figure 9.6 Structure for Conversation for Possibilities

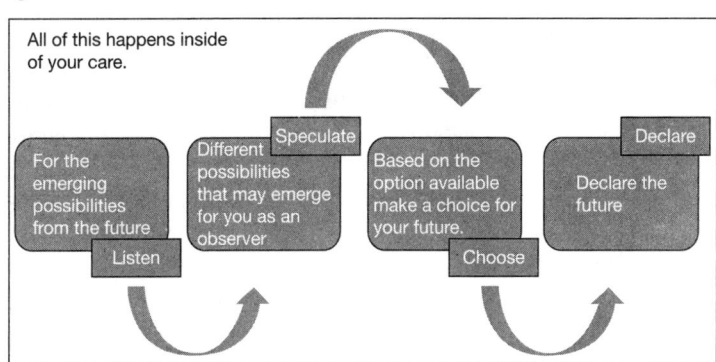

things. For example, there is a keyboard on which I am typing right now. If the keyboard did not exist, I would not be able to type. The keyboard is a real thing that exists irrespective of the observer. Possibilities are not like keyboards, that is, real things that you can touch and feel. Possibilities exist or do not exist depending on the observer you are. By definition, a possibility is not real. If we could prove it already exists, it would not be a possibility. They exist only in the eyes of the observer.

If you listen for possibilities, you will find possibilities—you just need to wear the lens to see these, and develop the ears to listen to these. Remember, when possibilities are over, possibilities are not over (*they were never really there in the first place*); it is from where you see (the observer you are) that they are over. If you tune yourself to listen for possibilities, you open up a space for possibilities to show up.

Speculate

According to Denning and Dunham, 'A speculation is a conversation in which the participants create new possibilities for future action, and set a context in which those actions make sense'. Speculative conversations relate to what could exist or might be done in the future. The key questions to be asked are, 'What is it possible to do?' 'What future would we like to create?' Or 'What new can we achieve or create?'[5]

The characteristics of speculation are

* openness to possibilities,
* no commitments to action and
* suspension of assessments.

The generative mood of speculation will be destroyed if participants are close-minded, inconsiderate to possible future action, overly critical of fragile new possibilities or too anxious to commit to a possibility. Participants who are in a speculation conversation do not assess prematurely, and let the possibilities live outside their automatic assessments of feasibility, relevance, value or success.

When speculative ideas are allowed to 'breathe', they may shift standards, and the way of looking at those ideas.

Choosing and Grounding Possibilities

Once you have completed the speculation, you can relax the no-criticism rule to begin sorting out the most encouraging possibilities.

To choose and ground possibilities, you can ask the following questions:

1. Do we care for this possibility?
2. Do we have history of achieving similar possibilities in the past; if not, can we trust our abilities to achieve these possibilities in the future?

People can have different grounding on the same situation of the same promise and they are just as valid; there's no right or wrong grounding. You could also say, 'I'm totally ungrounded here and I'm going to go forward anyway because I have an intuition, or I have a desire.'

So we do not want to overhype the value of the grounding, like it is going to give you the right answer; it does not. It is all judgement; it is all based on skill, but as you use this, it does help you see when you are unclear, you do not have clear standards and you are not really providing evidence.

Declaration

Most accomplishments begin when someone makes a declaration: 'This is possible'. Your missing action, or missing conversation, can be that of a declarative speech act, that is, of bringing forth a new future through the speech act of declaration.

While we constantly make declarations about what is or is not possible, we seldom do so responsibly. Every word we speak either expands options for action and brings forth a new future or guarantees the status quo, or even closes possibilities. Please refer to Chapter 5 for more information on declaration.

Summary and Reconstruction of Our Understanding

1. The common-sense understanding of action is that action is movement. Bob Dunham redefines action as 'acts that create subsequent behaviour and movement'. This is a generative meaning of the word 'action', and with this meaning of the word 'action', you may see that you can generate action for yourself, and also generate action in others. In this book, we have looked at actions as 'speech and listening actions' that you take, so that you create action for yourself and others.

2. Action is shaped by commitment—by the commitments we make or do not make, the clarity of the commitment and the ownership and importance of the commitment to the person committing.

3. At IGL, we claim that the *fundamental unit of work in organizations is the agreement*, not the task. Agreements are commitments. Where do these commitments come from? They always arise in conversations.

4. All results, both individually and socially, have as their root cause *prior conversations*, conversations which are had, conversations which are missing, conversations that are performed well or poorly. This is a powerful claim that emphasizes the pragmatic relevance of the generative perspective—that all results are ultimately shaped by conversations.

5. Conversations are not just language, but interactions that involve and are shaped by the body and emotions as well, and have a background of history and practice.

6. Our care determines what commitments have meaning for us.

7. If you do not have the results that you want, there are missing conversations that you need to distinguish first and then have—with others and with yourself.

8. If you 'listen' for dissatisfaction in and around your organization, you will begin to distinguish the missing or broken conversations. When faced with dissatisfaction, a

powerful question is: 'What conversations are missing that would produce a different result?'

9. Listening is an interpretation that the listener makes based on his or her context. The listening context of every individual is different, and hence, while the speaker says one thing, and if there are five listeners, each of the five listeners listen differently based on their individual context. The listening context of an individual is determined by his/her history, culture, practices, past assessments, body and moods and emotions.

10. Listening is a fundamental capacity of leadership. It is the background structure of interpretation that gives meaning to whatever we perceive. A key skill of listening is to accept that everyone listens differently.

11. This book claims 'You get what you "listen" for', and based on this, the book presents 4 important types of listening:

    a. *Listening to Make Yourself Right*
        As humans, we are assessment-making machines and we do not even realize that we make assessments, hold these to be the truth, forget we made this up and then *listen for evidence* to continuously and subconsciously validate this 'truth'.

    b. *Listening for Objective Facts*
        Leaders consciously look for objective facts, and do not always depend on their past assessments. Leaders look for assertions (objective facts) and then make grounded assessments. They do not depend on their past ungrounded assessments.

    c. *Listening for Care and Commitment*
        Action comes from commitment, and commitment comes from care. You can choose to listen for care and commitment of the other.

    d. *Listening for Possibilities*
        My claim is there are possibilities all around us, except most of us have not developed the eyes to see these possibilities and the ears to listen for these possibilities.

12. Leaders begin with conversations, and in conversations, they begin by first 'listening'. It is a myth that they begin conversations by speaking. They begin conversations by first choosing what they want to listen for. And they listen for

   - objective facts,
   - care and commitment and
   - possibilities.

13. There are several different types of conversations that you have with others. I am listing the important ones in the context of declaring breakdowns.

   - Conversation for relationships
   - Conversation for possibilities
   - Conversation for action

14. To get meaningful and productive results with other people, the first conversation you need to have is a *conversation for relationship*.

15. Conversations for relationship create a foundation of workability in which people are free to express their concerns and make open requests.

16. The objective of this conversation is to establish shared interest, shared care and shared commitment.

17. Conversation for possibility generates ideas for possible action. This conversation is conducted in a mood of curiosity, speculation and identifying possible future actions without judging them or committing to them.

18. The structure for conversations for possibilities includes the following elements:

   a. Listen
   b. Speculate
   c. Choose
   d. Declare

Generative Practices

1. What do you care about? If you have not identified your cares yet, this might be a good time to do so.
2. Remember, you take care of your cares when you have commitments in each of your cares, and you act inside of these commitments. What are your different commitments inside each of your cares (what results would you like to achieve in each of your cares)?
3. Practice the listening act. Actively choose any one from the following three types of listening when in conversation with yourself or with others:

   • Listening for objective facts
   • Listening for care and commitment
   • Listening for possibilities

4. Be present to when you are listening to make yourself right (or listening to make the other wrong).
5. In which of your relationships do you need to have a conversation for relationship? Have these conversations with them and journal what transpired?
6. By having these missing conversations for relationships with people, what conversations for possibility opened up for you? What new possible outcomes may be generated, which were not available to you earlier?

Include these questions as daily journaling questions to help you practise seeing the world with these distinctions, and to open new possibilities for your future.

Notes

1. Fernando Flores, 'Preface', in *Conversation for Action and Collected Essays: Instilling a Culture of Commitment in Working Relationships*, ed. Maria Flores (South Carolina: CreateSpace Independent Publishing Platform, 2012), ix.

2. Anatomy of action is a creation of Bob Dunham. He has referred to the anatomy of action in several of his papers, some unpublished. He has also referred to this in his paper 'The Generative Foundations of Action in Organizations: Speaking and Listening' published by the *International Journal of Coaching in Organisations* in 2009.

3. Teresa Amabile and Steven Kramer, 'How Leaders Kill Meaning at Work', *McKinsey Quarterly* (January 2012), http://www.mckinsey.com/insights/leading_in_the_21st_century/how_leaders_kill_meaning_at_work, accessed 17 February 2016.

4. Bob Dunham, 'The Generative Foundations of Action in Organisations: Speaking and Listening', *International Journal of Coaching in Organisations* 2 (2009).

5. Peter J. Denning and Robert Dunham, *The Innovator's Way* (Cambridge, MA: MIT Press, 2010).

10

Conversation for Action

In the earlier chapter, we looked at the anatomy of action, the listening act, conversation for relationships and the conversation for possibility, in identifying possible missing actions to be taken in achieving the new future you have created. Once you have had these important conversations, then comes the crucial conversation for action. The conversation for action is integral in managing and choreographing actions for the sake of achieving results that you desire, and in this case, the new future that you have created.

This could have had been a part of the earlier chapter, and is part of the Step 5 of declaring breakdowns. However, given the distinctiveness of this conversation, I have chosen to have a separate chapter dedicated to this conversation.

The conversation for action[1] is useful not only for declaring breakdowns but also for a crucial skill to learn for management. It is the structure for coordination of action. It is a non-discretionary structure. It is not just a technique, but is a structure that you will find in the world if you have the eyes to look for it. Conversations for actions are happening all around us. The question is, 'Are the conversations happening effectively and are these conversations generating the desired results?'

There is a clear structure to this conversation, and it is there for you to see, as long as you develop the eyes to see this structure, and a practice to embody this structure as a part of coordinating action and generating results.

Mastery in conversation for action will enable you to get things done, some of which you never earlier imagined were possible. There are seemingly simple elements to the conversation for action; however, my experience as a leadership coach has been that very few people have much competence in these speech acts. Lets us begin with some claims:

- Human action is shaped by commitment.
- Where there is no commitment, there will be no action (or the action will not happen the way it is meant to happen).
- People communicate and make commitments to each other in order to produce future actions, results and satisfaction. We call this *coordination of action.*
- Coordination of action is natural and is happening all the time. But it can be enhanced significantly if we become aware of how it is being generated and become observers of the coordination, actions and commitments.
- We produce our futures, both as individuals and as team, through our commitments.
- Coordination of action is the basis of producing results in business, and since coordination *costs*, the more effectively we coordinate, the more valuable our actions will be. We want to reduce the cost of coordination and increase the value produced by coordination.

We coordinate our actions to bring about something specific in the future by clarifying and making certain who is committed to doing what by when. We make promises for specific actions to specific people in specific time frames. We make requests of specific people for specific actions in specific time frames.

The conversation for action involves two parties, in the roles of what we call the 'customer' and the 'performer', who work together to negotiate a condition of satisfaction (COS) to which both commit to. The customer is a person who makes a request, and the performer is the one who responds to the request and may make a commitment (Figure 10.1). The key milestones in the conversation are as follows:

Figure 10.1 Steps 1 and 2 of Conversation for Action

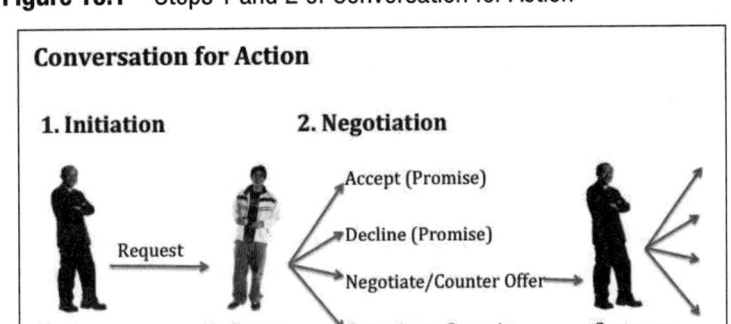

- *Request*: The customer makes a request and outlines the COS to the performer.
- *Negotiation*: The performer does one of four things: accepts, declines, counter-offers or commits to commit (defer).
- In the event of a counter-offer that the performer makes to the customer, the customer has the same four choices of accept, decline, counter-offer or commit to commit.
- *Promise*: After the negotiation, the performer makes a promise to perform.
- *Execution*: Performer performs.
- *Declaration of Completion*: Performer declares completion to the customer.
- *Declaration of Satisfaction*: Customer declares satisfaction (or dissatisfaction).
- *Revoke/Cancel*: During this process, the customer can revoke the request, or the performer can cancel the promise.

Speech and Listening Act: Request

The first question to be asked is, 'Why is a request made?'

Requests are made when we have an assessment that the future is going to unfold in a certain way, and that future is not what we want. We want a different future to come into existence, and for that we are committed to taking action. However, there are certain actions that we may not have the capacity to take; for example, we may not have the skill, or the authority or the resources or, for that matter, even time to take—however, we remain committed to that future. In such a case, we make a request to a person who in our assessment has the capacity to perform that action.

Requests are a structure that can include unlimited scale, for example, we can say 'please pass the ball' or 'invest in my organization a billion dollars for a business venture'. They have the same structure, but different COS.

Making effective requests is an important leadership move, and is an essential and unavoidable act in getting things done so that a new created future may be achieved. It seems very simple, and yet very few leaders know how to make effective requests. One of the biggest barriers to learning how to make effective requests is the hidden arrogance that I already know how to do so, or the assessment that given my position, I should already know this.

A claim that I can make with a fair amount of certainty based on my experience as a coach is that people usually do not even know that a missing action can be produced by perhaps a missing request that they can make of some person. A request is asking someone to perform, and this simple act can put into motion a series of actions leading to achieving a new future.

It is a skill to make effective requests. People fail to make effective requests and then wonder why the job did not get done well. As mentioned earlier, your results are a function of your actions. Actions are *acts that create commitment and subsequent movement*. One act that creates movement is 'making requests'; if you want results, you have to make effective requests.

The elements of effective requests are as follows:

- *Who* is making the request?
  Is the person (a committed customer) making the request committed to the fulfilment of the request? Is she/he a good customer? Does she/he take responsibility to work with the performer if she/he has any trouble? Or has she/he put the entire burden on the performer, ready to blame the performer for non-performance?

One of the key attributes of a committed customer is that a committed customer takes necessary actions to generate a committed performer. She/he then supports the performer to fulfil his/her request.

- *Of whom* is the request being made?
Is the request being made to a specific person (a committed performer), or is the request going to a group? Is the performer accepting the request only because she/he is afraid of declining the request? Is the performer acting out of his/her commitment to the request?

One of the key attributes of a committed performer is she/he is present and aware, and truly listens to the request. His/her body demonstrates interest to understand what you are speaking or requesting. A committed performer is committed to make agreements and fulfil them to satisfy the customer.

- *What* are the COS?
Results are not just the outcome of actions, but the assessment of satisfaction or dissatisfaction of the customer of the outcome.

There are two 'what' elements and this is the first of the two 'what' elements.

Whenever you request for some future action, you clarify the COS, that is, what are the conditions that will satisfy you when the other takes the action you request. This is one of the most common missing elements of a request. It is very common that the customer and the performer have different interpretations of the COS. If the customer and the performer do not agree on the COS, and the work begins anyway, a lot of hard work can go into the fulfilment of the request and yet the customer may not be satisfied because his/her conditions were not fulfilled. A relationship issue can develop between the customer and the performer only because the COS was not clearly established in the beginning. A shared commitment cannot exist unless there is a shared understanding.

- *What* is the shared background of obviousness?
This is the second of the two 'what' elements. The background of obviousness is what is listened that is not

said. This comes from the background and history of each listener, and is different for each person. A key skill of coordination and leadership is making sure we have a shared background for our requests and promises.

If the customer and the performer have not worked together much in the past, chances are they do not have a shared background of obviousness. The lesser the background of obviousness, the more the need to specify the COS. After working for several years with my team at IGL, we now have developed a reasonable background of obviousness. Despite that, I sometimes notice what is obvious to a colleague of mine is not obvious to me—and hence, at times, we still see the need to specify our COS to get the job done.

- *When* is the specified time for fulfilment?
  This is fairly straightforward; however, it is often not effectively used element of requests. 'When', or the time frame, can also be treated as a part of the COS. It has been listed separately because we notice people often use phrases such as 'as soon as possible', 'please attend to this immediately' or 'please look into this when convenient'.

  The customer presumes that it is 'obvious' she/he needs it to be done as soon as possible, while for the performer, the customer has stated 'please look into this when convenient' and she/he will look into this when convenient.

  Not being clear on the time for fulfilment is one of the most common breakdowns in coordination. The customer and the performer have different expectations of the 'when'— or the time of completion. It also leads to over-commitment. People avoid making clear commitments with specific times to avoid negotiations, having to decline, or to be honest about what can be really be done. This is an important focus for leaders in their conversations.

- *Why*: For the sake of what am I making this request?
  The *for the sake of what* element helps clarify what you care about, and what you are taking care of with this request.

  When the purpose of the request is included, that is, the 'for the sake of what am I making this request' element included, the request takes on a greater meaning. The performer understands the reason for the request and it helps in soliciting commitment from the performer.

- *How*: What is the mood of the person making the request? What mood do you want to generate in the person of whom you are making the request?

  You can include every element of the request as stated above, but if the mood of the request is not appropriate to the request being made, the request may be unfulfilled. The right conversation in the wrong mood will not give you the result you seek.

  While the customer certainly needs to make the request in the appropriate mood, she/he needs to be cognizant of the mood being generated in the performer.

A 'request' act is effective when the above elements have been included in the request. When you make the act of request with all these elements, the chances of your request being accepted and the job being done, as you would like it to be done, are greater. However, this does not guarantee that all your requests will be accepted and the job will be done as you would like it to be done.

Powerful Request

An effective request gets the performer to commit to the action. The act of a powerful request gets the performer to commit to a new (shared) future and then take actions inside of this new future. A powerful request goes beyond an effective request. It has all the elements of an effective request and more.

A powerful request is made when you create a new empowering (shared) future that connects with the other person and this person is touched, moved and inspired by this new empowering shared future. The person feels a shift in that moment that makes this person want to achieve the future you have created. A powerful request shows up as an opportunity to the other person and motivates the other person to make a commitment to that new future.

Powerful requests are powerful because they present a choice to the person. Until that moment, the other person did not have a choice of the (shared) future you created. You presented that choice to the other person.

To make a powerful request, you have to take on responsibility, that is, be willing to be the cause in the matter.

The Gift Your Organ Foundation made a powerful request to the health secretary in the Karnataka government to make organ donation as a part of the driver's licence. We at the Gift Your Organ Foundation did not know what request to make for action to the health secretary. We did not know how the internal government machinery operates. So, we made a powerful request to the health secretary, and showed him a future that this one move can create. Clearly, he was touched, moved and inspired by this new future, and committed to take whatever actions that were required to be taken, at his end, within the government.

We, on our part, committed to take actions to achieve this new shared future.

Unreasonable Request

As a coach, I have seen people getting stopped from making requests, which mean they have stopped themselves from taking action and participating actively in the causation of the future they created. The reason for doing so is that they assess their request to be unreasonable. Humans get stopped from achieving extraordinary success because they want to be reasonable. 'Unreasonable' is an assessment that you make, without realizing that you are making this assessment, and it is this assessment that stops you from making a request to the performer.

There are several automatic assessments that stop people from making requests, such as

- 'It's going to be declined anyway, so why make the request?'
- 'What will they think of me if I make this request?'
- 'I don't make these kinds of requests!'
- 'She is very busy and does not have the time for my requests.'
- 'I hate my requests being declined.'

I am sure there are many more similar assessments that make your requests appear unreasonable to you. These are all assessments that stop you from taking action, and hence stop you from achieving new results.

Recently, in my coaching conversation with a leader in a business unit of a global IT organization, it got disclosed that my coachee wanted to make a request to the President of his organization to set up a new business unit that would provide a support function to the organization itself. He thought this unit would help the organization save significant amounts of money. He had this thought for over a year, and never made the request, presuming it would be treated as unreasonable and would be declined.

Finally, in a coach call, he decided in the next one-to-one with the President, he would make the request. The President thought it was a great idea, and requested for a detailed proposal on this idea from him. My coachee was delighted with the response of the President.

My claim is when a person makes a request or an offer that he or she has historically not made, there is a certain expansion that takes place in that person. This expansion does not only happen if the request is accepted. It happens when the request is made, and is irrespective of the response to the request. There is a certain freedom in making a request that you have not made because it appeared as an unreasonable request up until that moment.

One of my favourite quotes of George Bernard Shaw is 'The reasonable man adapts himself to the world; the unreasonable one persists to adapt the world to himself. Therefore all progress depends on the unreasonable man.'

Speech and Listening Act: Offer

Offers are very similar to requests; however, in this case, the performer initiates and makes an offer to the customer. Once the customer accepts the performer's offer, it becomes the promise of the performer.

The effective offer act remains the same as the request act. 'Who', 'Whom', 'What', 'When', 'Why' and 'How' are questions that apply to effective offers too.

Your missing action may be a missing offer that can change the course of the future and lead you to a new future of your creation.

Negotiation

Negotiation is the process that takes place after the request or offer has been made, and before an agreement has been arrived at between the customer and the performer. The performer in case of a request and customer in case of an offer can have 4 possible responses to a request or offer:

1. Accept
2. Decline
3. Negotiate
4. Commit to commit

Each of these are totally valid responses. Unfortunately, the common sense in much of the world is that a 'decline' to a request is not an acceptable response. My claim is that a 'decline' is as valid a response as an 'accept' is. I would rather have a 'decline' than have an 'accept' and then have the performer not perform. We are looking for commitment in our interactions with others. Promise or decline show the commitment of the other person and show us the future that we share together. A promise that is really a hidden decline is a breakdown coming.

When there is decline, many people make it that the 'person and their care has been declined'. This is certainly not the case—it is not the person or their care that has been rejected, it is the request that has been declined. The person making the request is distinct from the request. When a request is declined, the person is not declined. If you embody this distinction, you will not be stopped from making requests (including unreasonable requests) to people.

When one performer declines, it does not mean that all performers will decline your request. I have noticed that people start to question their request and make their request unreasonable when a performer declines the request. You can most definitely make the same request to another performer, who may offer a different response.

And finally, my experience has been that a decline to a request is a decline in that moment. It does not stop you from making the same request at another time to the same performer. Out of experience, I can state that my requests have been accepted by the same performer who initially declined my request. The request was made again at a different moment in time, and at that time, the performer accepted my request.

Speech and Listening Act: Promise

Several times in this book, we have claimed that results are a function of action. If we want new results, we certainly need to take actions. In section 'Anatomy of Action' in the previous chapter, we also claimed that *action is shaped by commitments*—the commitments we make or do not make, the clarity of the commitment and the ownership and importance of the commitment to the person or organization committing.

In effect, what we are saying is when you make a request, you are looking to produce a commitment or a promise that you can trust. If not, as a part of declaring breakdowns, you may have declared a great new future, made an effective request and yet not achieved this new future. This is because the people you need support from were not committed to action.

When you take responsibility, you become the cause of soliciting trustworthy commitments (by making effective requests), from your network of support.

For the purposes of this book, we will use the words 'promise' and 'commitment' interchangeably. According to Chalmers Brothers,[2] 'our whole social fabric and structure, our whole economic network, are held together by promises—promises between businesses and organisations, as well as those between individuals'.

Brothers adds, 'promises and agreements and commitments underlie everything that we do with others. They are the most basic level, the "actual action" that we use in very different ways, as we do what we do in the world'.

So, what is a promise or a commitment?

A promise or a commitment is an act that is distinguished by a listener that someone, a promisor, is committing to produce some future action or result.

A promise is founded in listening, and exists only in listening. By this we mean that someone who says 'promise' does not produce a promise unless the utterance produces the listening of 'promise' in others. Similarly, the listener may listen to a promise, even when the promisor did not make an explicit promise. For example, my daughter makes a request to me that we watch a movie on the weekend. I respond back stating, 'OK, let's see on Sunday'.

My daughter gets excited, presuming her dad said 'yes' to her request. While, in my understanding, I said, 'We will see on Sunday', meaning thereby we will decide on Sunday. So, for my daughter, there is a promise, and as far as I am concerned, I have not made a promise. Our claim is that promise exists in the listening of the listener. If we do not keep our promise, as listened by the listener, the listener will not trust us in the future. It will impact the relationship with the listener, and eventually will impact the success and public identity of the concerned promisor.

What is key to understand is that a promise from a performer changes the world of the customer in the now, not after the execution and completion of the promise. The customer now trusts that you will take care of this matter and she/he can now choose to take care of another matter, engage in some other endeavour. From the earlier example, one can deduce that my daughter got excited in the moment when she thought she had a promise from her father.

To manage action is to manage promises. If promises are not shifted, then neither will the action be shifted.

To manage a promise is to

- keep the customer informed, on a regular basis;
- tell the customer if there is an interruption, and let them know what you are still promising;
- navigate and produce a new plan and set of actions;
- be prepared to modify or make new promises;
- declare 'complete' when you have fulfilled the promise;
- ask the customer if they are satisfied; and
- determine if there are new offers you can make.

Figure 10.2   Step 3 of Conversation for Action

Declaration of Completion

When the performer performs the action, it is important that the performer performs per the COS agreed between the customer and the performer. During the process of performing the action, it is important that the performer remains in touch with the customer and keeps the customer updated on unexpected delays or changes.

Once the performance stage is completed, the performer declares completion to the customer. It can be in the form of stating 'It's complete' or 'I've done the actions you requested', or submitting any report that was part of the COS.

In my experience as a coach, I have noticed this is a common missing conversation in conversations for action (Figure 10.2).

Declaration of Satisfaction

Once the performer declares completion, there is one more step in the completion of the entire conversation for action and that is the declaration of satisfaction by the customer to the performer. This declaration of satisfaction is usually just a simple 'thank you' (Figure 10.3).

Figure 10.3   Step 4 of Conversation for Action

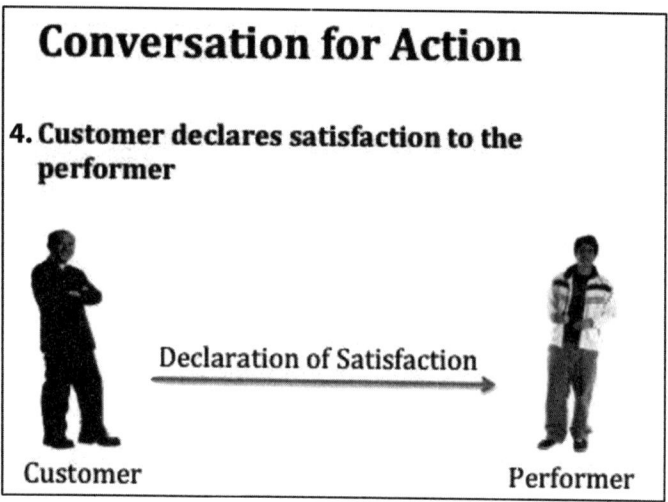

In certain cases, the customer may not be satisfied with the performer's actions, and in such a case, the entire conversation for action may be re-initiated.

An important skill to be developed is to separate out the conversations for relationships, conversations for possibilities and the conversations for action, and to know when the time is right to move from one conversation to the other. The transition is marked by a shift in the mood. The ideal mood of the conversation for relationship is curiosity, the ideal mood for the conversation for possibilities is speculation and the ideal mood for conversation for action resolution.

Summary and Reconstruction of Our Understanding

1. To achieve the new created future, we need to identify missing conversations for action, and then choreograph these actions effectively with others.

2. The conversation for action involves two parties, the customer and the performer, who work together to negotiate a COS that to which both commit to.

3. The customer is a person who makes a request, and the performer is the one who makes a commitment. The key milestones in the conversation are as follows:

   a. *Request*: The customer makes a request and outlines the COS to the performer.

   b. *Negotiation*: The performer does one of four things: accepts, declines, counter-offers or commits to commit (defer).

   c. In the event of a counter-offer that the performer makes to the customer, the customer has the same four choices of accept, decline, counter-offer or commit to commit.

   d. *Promise*: After the negotiation, the performer makes a promise to perform.

   e. *Execution*: Performer performs.

   f. *Declaration of Completion*: Performer declares completion to the customer.

   g. *Declaration of Satisfaction*: Customer declares satisfaction (or dissatisfaction).

   h. *Revoke/Cancel*: During this process, the customer can revoke the request, or the performer can cancel the promise.

4. Requests are made when we have an assessment that the future is going to unfold in a certain way, and that future is not what we want. We want a different future to come into existence, and for that we are committed to taking action. However, there are certain actions that we may not have the capacity to take. In such a case, we make a request to a person who in our assessment has the capacity to perform that action.

5. Making effective requests is an important leadership move, and is the biggest and the most useful act in getting things done so that a new created future may be achieved.

6. It is a skill to make effective requests. People fail to make effective requests and then wonder why the job did not get done well.

7. The elements of effective requests:

a. *Who* is making the request?

   i. Is the person making a request committed to the fulfilment of the request?

b. *Of Whom* is the request being made?

   i. Is a request being made to a specific person (a committed performer), or is a request going to a group? Is the performer accepting a request only because she/he is afraid of declining the request? Is the performer acting out of his/her commitment to the request?

c. *What* are the COS?

   i. There are two 'what' elements and this is the first of the two 'what' elements.

   ii. Whenever you request for some future action, you clarify the COS, that is, what are the conditions that will satisfy you when the other takes the action you request. This is one of the most common missing elements of a request. It is very common that the customer and the performer have different interpretations of the COS.

d. *What* is the shared background of obviousness?

   i. This is the second of the two 'what' elements. What is the background of obviousness between the speaker and the listener?

   ii. If the customer and the performer have not worked together much in the past, chances are they do not have a shared background of obviousness. The lesser the background of obviousness, the more the need to specify the COS.

e. *When* is the specified time for fulfilment?

   i. 'When', or the time frame, can also be treated as a part of the COS. It has been listed separately because we notice people often use phrases such as 'as soon as possible', 'please attend to this immediately' or 'please look into this when convenient'.

f. *Why*: For the sake of what am I making this request?

    i. When the purpose of the request is included, that is, the 'for the sake of what am I making this request' element included, the request takes on a greater meaning. The performer understands the reason for the request and it helps in soliciting commitment from the performer.

g. *How*: What is the mood of the person making the request? What mood do you want to generate in the person of whom you are making the request?

8. An effective request gets the performer to make a trustworthy commitment to action. A powerful request gets the performer to commit to a new (shared) future and then take actions inside of this new future. A powerful request goes beyond an effective request. It has all the elements of an effective request and more.

9. You can have 4 possible responses to a request:

a. Accept
b. Decline
c. Negotiate
d. Commit to commit

10. Each of these is totally valid responses. Unfortunately, the common sense in much of the world is that a 'decline' to a request is not an acceptable response. My claim is that a 'decline' is as valid a response as an 'accept' is. I would rather have a 'decline' than have an 'accept' and then have the performer not perform.

11. A promise is an act that is distinguished by a listener that someone, a promisor, is committing to produce some future result.

12. To manage action is to manage promises. If promises are not shifted, then neither will the action be shifted. Managing action and managing promises is done in conversations.

13. The performer performs the action, and it is important that the performer performs as per the COS agreed between the customer and the performer. During the

process of performing the action, it is important that the performer remains in touch with the customer and keeps the customer updated on unexpected delays or changes.

14. Once the performance stage is completed, the performer declares completion to the customer. It can be in the form of stating 'It's complete' or 'I've done the actions you requested', or submitting any report that was part of the COS.

15. Once the performer declares completion, there is one more step in the completion of the entire conversation for action and that is the declaration of satisfaction by the customer to the performer. This declaration of satisfaction is usually just a simple 'thank you'.

Generative Practices

1. Are you making effective requests? What elements of requests are generally missing for you?

2. Use these elements of effective requests and see how this impacts the response to the request (making effective requests does not guarantee a trustworthy commitment—it certainly increases the chances of receiving a trustworthy commitment).

3. If *action is shaped by commitment*, a question for you to reflect upon is: 'Are you committed to action, or are you committed to comfort?' What action are you committed to, inside of achieving a new future in each of your cares? Please journal your responses. We often avoid honest conversations and commitments to stay in our comfort zones. This often limits our impact as leaders.

4. What do you do when you make a request and receive a commitment that you cannot trust? Do you accept this untrustworthy commitment? You have a choice to let the person know that you do not trust his/her commitment, and seek a commitment that you can trust.

5. What does 'promise exists in the listening of the other' provoke in you? Do you agree with this statement? A place

to look at is when you were a listener and listened to a promise, when the other person did not make an explicit promise. How did you feel when that promise (which in the eyes of the promisor was not even a promise) was not kept? Did you feel let down? Did you lose trust in the promisor? What was the impact on your relationship?

The same thing holds true for your promises. These exist in the listening of the listener. Please journal your reflections, and new possible actions.

6. As a performer, do you declare completion, and as a customer, do you declare satisfaction? If not, reflect on what may be the impact of not doing so.

Use these questions for daily journaling, for the sake of improving your capacity to create the future with others that you are committed to and care about.

Notes

1. I have referred to the work of Fernando Flores on this topic. He has a book titled *Conversations for Action and Collected Essays: Instilling a Culture of Commitment in Working Relationships*, edited by Maria Flores Letelier (South Carolina: CreateSpace Publishing Platform, 2013).
2. Chalmers Brothers, *Language and the Pursuit of Happiness* (Florida: New Possibilities Press, 2005).

11
Execution

The sixth and the last step of declaring breakdowns is 'execution'. Once you have identified the missing actions, you execute the actions. This book is about getting skilled in the conversation of declaring breakdowns, and taking the missing conversational actions in achieving the future you create.

Without execution, you will not achieve the future you have created. In the chapter on identifying missing actions, we have already gone deep into the conversational actions that may be missing. This book does not dwell much in the domain of execution after the conversational action is taken, and presumes you are already skilled in executing action relating to your domain. And if you are not, you have a choice to declare a breakdown and create a future to get skilled in your domain by following the steps listed in the book.

So that you make execution an important step for your life too, following are some thoughts for your practice to develop skills in execution.

Performance Happens 'on the Court'

Are you 'on the court' as far as your own life is concerned? Are you executing actions to deliver on your promises?

Most people I interact with regularly keep saying things like 'I have wanted to go to the gymnasium for so many months now but just cannot get myself to' or 'I have been planning to start my business but am waiting for the right opportunity.

'Being on the court' means making and fulfilling promises and not wondering what people around you are saying. Listening to too many other assessments (including the internal chatter of your mind) can shake your conviction and take you off your course.

Then there are other people who do get on to the court, but seek approval, assurance and views from the 'people in the stands'. It is fine to seek others' views, and that actually is a great idea. However, the views that are important are that of your coach, teammates, captain (read 'manager') and so on. Certainly not of the 'people in the stands'. (*And if you do not have a coach yet, seriously consider getting one.*)

'Being on the court' means being the cause in the matter. Remember, it is actions you take that lead to your performance. History is evidence of the fact that no one has ever won the game by being in the stands.

The problem for a lot of people is not that they do not know what to do; the problem is that they simply do not do it.

> It is important that you get clear for yourself that your only access to impacting life is action. The world does not care what you intend, how committed you are, how you feel or what you think, and certainly it has no interest in what you want and don't want. Take a look at life and see for yourself that the world only moves for you when you act. (Werner Erhard)

Transform Your Relationship with Failure

Roger Martin, in his article in the *Harvard Business Review*,[1] stated,

> Most people agree that the two strongest human urges are survival and procreation, but there is very little consensus on the next most powerful. I believe it's the need to succeed. Humans hate to fail—hate it more than almost anything else.

He adds:

> If you hate failure, you have a wonderful way of ensuring that you don't experience it: Play the game you know you can win. Think about it. On one hand, you can tackle a difficult challenge and face the prospect of failing. On the other, you can strive for a manageable goal and pretty much guarantee that you'll achieve it. I would argue that most people systematically choose the second course of action.

I have experienced this phenomenon of people being in inaction, because of the fear of failure. As Werner Erhard states, 'Your only access to impacting life is action, and hence to achieve the future you have created, your only access is action'.

I invite you to transform your relationship with failure, and for that you need to understand what failure is.

So, what is failure?

Failure is the product of a conversation you have with yourself. By now, you know the distinction between assertions and assessments, and failure is an assessment—it is an assessment that what you wanted to achieve was not achieved. Failure is not an assertion.

The reason I am bringing out the conversation of your relationship with failure here is because many people very easily give up on their created future. They give up because in the first, second or the third attempt, they did not achieve what they set out to achieve. They create a story that 'this will never work', or 'I am a failure—I can never achieve this', or so forth.

We do not ever have to give up our care, our commitment or our possibilities. We can take every moment as a moment of choice where we can start again in creating our future. We can always open a new conversation, enter a new mood, shift our perspective or change our standards. We can always create, we can always generate, whatever the situation.

As humans, we were created to be unstoppable, and I have evidence of this in my home. My wife and I recently became parents of gorgeous twins. These twins were born premature, but have been unstoppable from the time of their birth (actually, from the time they were conceived!). I am seeing them grow week after week. First, they would not recognize us, but now they do; earlier, they could not hold their necks straight, but now they do.

As they grow older, they will first learn to turn while lying down. Once they have turned and come on their stomachs, they will not be able to go back to their earlier position of lying on their back. They will yell for help and one of us will have to straighten them. But, they will not learn from this 'mistake'—they will do the same thing again and again and again, till they learn to turn back on their own.

And then they will learn to sit up, and then to crawl. While crawling, they will fall a number of times, hurt themselves and yet not stop. Eventually, they will master crawling. Again, thankfully, that will not be enough for them.

They will want to learn to walk, run, cycle, swim and so on. And each time, they will fall several times, possibly even harming themselves. Yet, they will not give up.

It is interesting that as we grow older, we think we become smarter, and yet this smartness works against us. We start to apply reason (read 'we start to make assessments') and make decisions that do not help us. If we fall (read 'fail'), we create such convincing reasons for not attempting again.

Failure is simply an assessment of a moment where our expectations were not fulfilled. But we still have a future, and a rich one.

In a workshop that I conducted recently for a large multinational organization, there was a practice that I asked the participants to do first thing in the morning of day 3. A senior manager in this organization could not complete the practice. He 'decided' that he was 'slow' and hence he could not complete the practice.

To me, he did not seem slow at all—he was active in the conversations during the programme. It was clear that the other participants had high regard for him, and his achievements. However, it was evident that he believed completely that he was 'slow', and him being slow was the reason for not completing the practice. My guess is that the practice was not completed because subconsciously he was proving himself to be right—that he was 'slow'.

And according to him because he 'is' slow, he does not make big promises. And when you do not make big promises, you do not have to execute on these promises.

Your many attempts can fail, and that is fine. The problem arises when you stop making attempts due to failure! The choice is between inaction and failure! For me, it is a no-brainer! I would much rather choose failure. The more you reside in inaction, the more you engage in conversation of wanting to avoid failure!

Make failure a lesson and an opening for the next step, not a block to the journey to your future. As long as you have breath and choice, you can create your journey to the future, and in fact always are doing so (your actions are creating your future, and so are your inactions).

Another reason people do not take action is because they are confused about what next to do.

Is Your Confusion an Indulgence?

'Sameer, I really am confused! Shall I take up a job or ensure my kids do well in school by being at home and taking care of their needs,' said one of my coaching clients. This had been the state with this lady not being able to make up her mind for over 2 years.

Another person I met at a training programme stated, 'I have been thinking of setting up a business for over a year and a half. I cannot decide what to do. What do you suggest?'

I hear people regularly say that they are confused. Confusion to me is an indulgence; a seemingly great place for some people to be because it gives them an excuse for taking no action. 'I am confused and if I am confused, how can I take any action? I need clarity before I can take any action!' said one of the students in a placement meeting at the business school that I used to head.

Confusion leads to inaction and inaction in turn leads to further confusion. This is a vicious circle that you want to avoid (Figure 11.1). Once you get into the mode of confusion, the spiral is downwards and difficult to escape.

I have noticed this about my life. Every time I have been confused, I realize I have been inactive. Even if it is for a few

Figure 11.1   Confusion–Inaction Vicious Circle

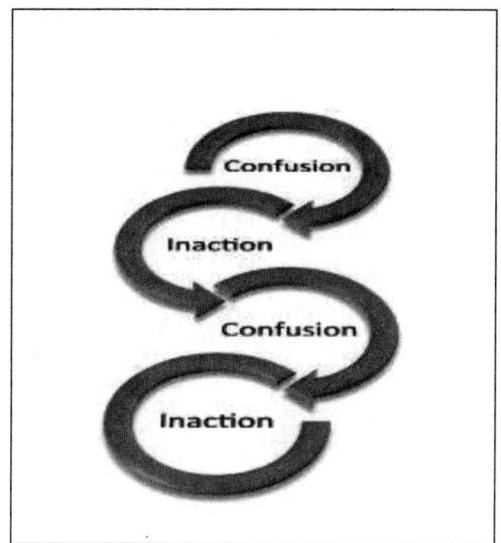

moments. The key is to brand my inaction as 'inaction' rather than call it 'confusion'. That way you know you are 'not in action'. And that to me is perfectly OK. There have been days I just have not felt like working. And I prefer saying it as it is—that I do not feel like working today.

In my interactions with several working executives, I notice they romanticize their inaction by calling it confusion. Once you have branded your inaction as confusion, you now have a very good reason for remaining in inaction. 'You are confused after all!' And how can confused people ever be asked to take any action? Here starts the never-ending downward spiral of confusion and inaction.

Here is something else for you to consider:

Confusion = Irresponsibility

Being responsible is being chargeable for being the author, for being the cause. You simply cannot cause anything in the state of confusion. To be the cause, you need to have clarity, distinctiveness; clarity and distinctiveness are functions of action.

How many times have you noticed that clarity automatically emerges when you take that elusive first step?

Which is why I have no hesitation in stating that confusion also means irresponsibility, in that you are not ready to take responsibility for the way things are right now and do what is required to be done to make the situation the way you want it to be.

Recently, while travelling with a friend in his car, we came across a junction where the traffic lights had just stopped working. Cars from all directions had started to create a jam and, in a very short while, it became a deadlock. Imagine this picture of the deadlock and now consider this to be the state of mind of a confused person.

I got out of the car, identified one car (someone else in my place may have identified another car—the point is not which car; the point is *one car* was identified) and requested that car to back up. As soon as that car backed up, another car from the opposite direction was able to move. With this, a little space got created and gradually the traffic opened up and we were able move past that jam in a matter of a few minutes. This traffic jam could otherwise easily have lasted an hour or more.

Therefore, the next time you are confused, consider doing the following:

- First and foremost, notice that you are not in action. Awareness will give you a choice to either get into action or remain in inaction.
- If you have phrased your inaction as confusion, rephrase 'I am confused' to 'I am not in action currently'—it means the same thing; however, the first statement gives you an excuse to remain in inaction, while the second statement acknowledges that you are not in action and that you will soon get back into action. By action, I do not necessarily mean doing things physically. *Applying thought is also being in action.* Get into action and start identifying and evaluating options.
- And finally, take that first step. Remember, from the earlier story, it does not matter what that first step is (which car is asked to move first). Take that step! Different people will take different first steps. And that is perfectly OK.

Keep in mind—those who take responsibility for their lives do not choose confusion. They are the cause of clarity in their lives and in the lives of others around them. And in those rare moments of confusion, they jump right back into action.

Get into Rhythm

'It takes about 20 years of doing the mundane to get on to the front page of *Economic Times*,' said Dr Ajoy Kumar in his 'CEO of the Month' lecture to the students of my institute about 15 years ago. This was the first 'CEO of the Month' session we had conducted and had invited Dr Kumar, then the CEO of one of the Cummins companies in India. (*For your information, Dr Ajoy Kumar is a Medical Doctor by qualification, who gave up medicine for pursuing the IPS (Indian Police Service) and became the Superintendent of Police of Jamshedpur and then gave that up for a corporate job.*)

While writing this book, I looked up to see where Dr Kumar is now and, not so surprisingly, found out that he is the Member of Parliament from Jamshedpur and is also the CEO of Max Neeman! (*I would love to write about Dr Kumar separately someday soon—he has a fascinating story.*)

My daughter does the mundane chores every day, and perhaps that is the reason for her success as a child. A few weeks back, I noticed that my 9-year-old daughter has quite a schedule—wake up at 6:45 AM; have breakfast, get ready, go to school, a fixed time table at school, return from school, go for either guitar classes or skating classes or chess classes, play down in the park for about 45 minutes and spend time with her mom and dad before getting to bed a few minutes before 8:30 PM. This has been her schedule every school day for the last 2 years and chances are that it will remain the same for the next 8 years before a new schedule takes over when she gets to college.

What a rhythm my daughter has found for herself! She knows exactly what she will be doing at what time of the day/week. She does not need much of a calendar to remind her of her rhythm. In this world obsessed with desires for new excitement soon after the last one is over, the observation of my daughter's rhythm of life came to me as a welcome change!

There are rhythms happening all the time: the heartbeat rhythm, day-and-night rhythm, the rhythm of the seasons, rush-hour rhythm, sleeping-and-waking-up rhythm and many more. These are all happening.

From the point of view of executing action, one way to do so is to establish rhythms around your conversations.

Rhythms of conversations are important, because, in effect, these are rhythms of actions that you take to generate a certain desired result. Every managerial role in an organization needs to have a certain set of conversations. Whether or not these conversations are had, and how effectively these conversations are had, will determine the success of the individual in that role, and the success of his/her team.

For example, the human resources head of an organization has a certain rhythm of conversations, which are distinct from the rhythm of conversations had by the public relations head, or the marketing head of the same organization. Each of these roles is meant to have regular conversations with a certain set of people.

When you create a rhythm around these conversations, you really foresee possible interruptions that may take place, and you avoid those interruptions from taking place.

I am inviting you to set up a rhythm of conversation that you have with yourself, and with key people in your team, organization or life.

Josephina Santiago, an acknowledged Somatic Program Leader and Coach, once asked me, 'Sameer, does the rhythm you are in currently support you?' This question made me stop and think.

'A certain rhythm may have served you at one point of time. Does that rhythm serve you today?' Josephina added.

What she meant to ask me was, 'Sameer, are you in a default flow of rhythms, those that served you at one moment of time, and may just not be serving you anymore?' If that is the case, then there is a default future that these rhythms are leading you to. Are you OK with this default future?

If yes, good.

If not, then design new rhythms, take new actions and generate a new future.

As a final point, I ask you the same question: 'Do your current rhythms support you in generating the future you desire?'

Summary and Reconstruction of Our Understanding

1. 'Being on the court' means being in action and not wondering what people around you are saying. Listening to too many (including the internal chatter of your mind) will shake your conviction and take you off your course.
2. 'Being on the court' means being the cause in the matter. Remember, it is actions you take that lead to your performance. History is evidence of the fact that no one has ever won the game by being in the stands.
3. Failure is an assessment—it is an assessment that what you wanted to achieve was not achieved. Failure is not an assertion.
4. A claim: confusion is an indulgence; a seemingly great place for some people to be because it gives them an excuse for taking no action.
5. Confusion leads to inaction and inaction in turn leads to further confusion. This is a vicious circle.
6. A rhythm of conversation is a rhythm of action that you take regularly to generate desired results. These rhythms are also created foreseeing possible interruptions and to avoid these interruptions from happening.

Generative Practices

1. Remember, 'performance happens on the court'. Where in your life are you not on the court, but on the stands? What is missing?
2. What is your relationship with failure? Get present to the assertions and the assessments, and remember, 'failure' is only a conversation.
3. Reflect and journal the existing rhythms that you have currently in your life.

4. What new rhythms (of conversations and other rhythms) can you create for your life? For example, a rhythm for your sales conversation, a rhythm for your workout and a rhythm for spending quality time with your family.
5. Take these questions for daily entries in your journal. Let them shape what you pay attention to, and reshape your actions and results.

Note

1. Roger Martin, 'Are You Confusing Strategy with Planning', *Harvard Business Review*, 2 May 2014. https://hbr.org/2014/05/are-you-confusing-strategy-with-planning/, accessed 16 February 2016.

Epilogue

The promise of this book was to provide knowledge of how to declare breakdowns. The promise was also to provide a platform to get skilled in declaring and dealing with breakdowns effectively through the practices listed at the end of each of the chapters. I am hoping I have kept this promise to you. If you have questions and concerns, you can visit our website www.declaringbreakdowns.com and my team and I will be delighted to respond to your specific concerns or questions.

This is the launch moment; you now know about declaring breakdowns, but the muscle needs to be developed. This muscle will be developed by actively participating in your life, declaring breakdowns where there is an interruption, or where you sense a disharmony, and also by creating and achieving futures of your choice. Your learning will be incomplete if you stop at reading this book, and not practise declaring breakdowns regularly in your life. This is where the rubber meets the road.

This is the first moment of the rest of your life! Right now, you have a choice. To be in drift, or be at the source of design of your life. What has happened, has happened. What is, is. Right now, like every moment of your life, you have a choice to create a new future. You have a choice to declare a breakdown.

I am inviting you to reflect on some of these questions. These are questions that I had asked you in the generative practices at the end of some of the chapters. There are no final answers to these questions.

1. What do you care about?
2. Are you satisfied with how you are taking care of your cares?
3. If no new action is taken, what is likely to happen in this area of your care in the foreseeable future?
4. Does this default future work for you?
5. If the default future does not work for you, what new future would you like to create in this area of your care?
6. Are you taking responsibility in achieving this new future, or, in other words, will you cause this future to happen?
7. What is the next missing conversational action for making this future happen? Is there a missing commitment (promise), or a missing request, or any other missing conversational action?

Once you have answered the above questions, go ahead and execute.

Please share your feedback with me on the comments page of our website www.declaringbreakdowns.com, or email me at sameer@sameerdua.com.

I am inviting you to regularly ask yourself these questions. It is the questions that you ask that will determine the answers that you get. It is the answers that you get that will determine the actions you will take, and that will determine the results that you have.

As I stated earlier:

Whether you agree with gravity or not, whether you like it or not, it has an impact in your life. Similarly, whether you know it or not, accept it or reject it, you are engaged in a constant process of creating your future.

Like every moment, here is your leadership moment. Here is an invitation to your choice. Go ahead and *create your future*!

Appendix 1: Old Interpretation to New Interpretation

Old Interpretation	New Interpretation
Breakdowns happen to us, and they are not good.	In generative language, breakdowns are created through an act of declaration. Interruptions happen to us, and we may choose to declare a breakdown. Interruptions are not good or bad. Our claim is that interruptions are nothing but a break in your transparency. An interruption disrupts the 'established order', and this established order was transparent till the 'interruption' took place. An interruption implies a change in your space of possibilities. What we assumed was possible before may no longer be possible or what we assumed may not be possible before may suddenly become a possibility. When you declare a breakdown, you actively participate in the process of designing a future of your choice.
Learning is knowing and understanding.	Learning means to shift embodiment (*what our body can see, attend, do* and *experience habitually*), and shift our capacity for action and outcomes.
Learning happens when we learn in our heads through concepts and knowledge.	Learning happens through practice. The body is a place of deep learning. In order to go beyond understanding and concepts as learning, we must learn through embodiment to achieve new skills, new perspectives and new ways to experience. Learning is happening already through practice. We are learning what we are practising.

(*Continued*)

(*Continued*)

Old Interpretation	New Interpretation
Practice is done by sportspersons, musicians, artists and so on. However, for leaders, once we have the knowledge, we can deliver.	Leadership is a performance art. To learn leadership, we need to know the concepts (the science), and then practise to become masterful in the art. One way of engaging with life and the world is through abstractions, thinking and reflections, but the mastery of action is always from embodied skill.
The common-sense understanding of a conversation is speaking and hearing. Most people presume beyond speaking and hearing, there is not much going on in a conversation.	Conversation is the interaction of human beings that creates action, meaning, listening, moods and emotions and connection with others and the future. Conversations are not just words, but the whole body reactions that are provoked when we interact in language, and when we interact and language is provoked. Conversations include language, moods and emotions, body reactions and experiences and the listening that is based on the history of the people in the conversation. Conversations are shaped in linguistic and cultural practices.
Communication is for transmission of information.	Communication is about sharing a world, cares and creating a shared future. Communication is 'changing together', and each person brings their worldview, background and presence to each conversation—it is a place of contact where the future is always being created through interaction (and even in silence).
One way that language is understood in our current age is as a description of our world, a set of labels that we use to describe things and people, a medium for the transfer of information. Much research in language has worked in this framework—that words correspond to entities and phenomena in the world. We see that a word like 'chair' corresponds to an artefact by that name in the world.	While our old interpretation works, it hides that language is generative, and highly creative—not just descriptive. Language has the power, and through language, we generate • action, • outcomes of action, • possibilities, • commitments, • identities, • opinions, • moods and emotions and much more.

Old Interpretation	New Interpretation
Language is of interest to academics, linguists, English teachers and so on.	Understanding and using the generative power of language is extremely important in the way we 'be' and operate. We are always living in language, and it is generative language where we establish how we see the world, what actions we take and how we coordinate with others. Language shapes our lives and the outcomes we produce.
We are pretty much aware of what is happening with us, and around us.	We all operate in some or other blindness. The unconscious performance of the body, or our habitual actions, or the way we see the world are great examples of what is transparent to us. What is transparent to us does not mean it is not happening. It is happening and yet is transparent to us. We are not aware of it. We do not have our attention on it. Every person and every tradition have their own awareness and blindness, where they put attention and where they do not.
The world we observe is the way the world is—what we see is what there is.	The world we see is a function of the observer we are. We are all caught up in our own worlds, that is, the world we observe, such that we do not even know that we do not know that there is a world beyond the one that we manifest. Every individual has a world that is different than anyone else's. This provides the power and richness of diversity, culture and possibility when we begin to share our worlds. There is no world without an observer, and if someone tries to describe such a world, they are 'that' observer.
What we observe is a function of what we look at (the attention to the observer is absent here).	'The observers we are' is a function of our language, emotion, body, history and culture and practice. Each person sees differently, and although some perspectives overlap, there is always a difference.

(Continued)

(*Continued*)

Old Interpretation	New Interpretation
The common-sense understanding of our culture is that the world we see is a function of what is 'out there'.	The world we see is a function of the observer we are. We live in two worlds, one is the physical world, and the other is the linguistic world that we create and manifest. The physical world is the same for everyone. However, it is this linguistic world that we create that determines • how we show up in the world, • what actions we take and • what results we have.
The world is what it is and we have no impact on it.	We create our world. And we are creating our world, whether or not we are aware of it; it is extremely powerful to learn how to create our worlds because awareness creates choice.
There is one way of seeing things, and it is only my way.	There are as many ways of seeing things as there are observers.
We live in the world.	We live in language. We create the world through our interpretations and how we see it. Our world is always a world of our interpretations.
We are who we are (you are fixed).	We are who we create ourselves to be—moment to moment. And we are doing this anyway, including when we live in the story that we are not.
Results are an outcome of the actions we take.	Indeed. Results are indeed a function of the actions we take. However, the actions we take are a function of the observer we are.
We have opinions, judgements and assessments.	That is right. However, sometimes our opinions, judgements and assessments have gotten us. Our lives are being driven by these opinions, judgements and assessments and we may be blind to this. We can become aware of our automatic judgements to design ones that serve our purpose.

Old Interpretation	New Interpretation
Responsibility is the state or fact of being answerable or accountable for something within one's power, or control.	To be responsible is to take the posture that we are the source or cause of something, we are open to be held accountable for the outcomes, we hold ourselves accountable for the outcomes and the outcomes can be shifted by our actions. Responsibility is a matter of our choice. It is making the interpretation that when we assess something is not working, we will provide what is missing to make it work. This puts us in the posture of producing action, not waiting for someone else to take action. It puts us in the posture of being a leader. We may not know what to do, but in this posture, we will find out, or invent, what is needed. If we wait for others or act only if we know what to do, we become a victim and paralyse ourselves with the reasons for our inaction and our lack of performance.
A team is a number of persons coming together for a joint action and for working together.	A team is number of persons coming together to fulfil a shared promise. A team exists to make and fulfil promises that individuals cannot fulfil.
The future is not in our control. We have no choice in creating our future; it comes to us.	The future is a function of our creation. We create our future through our declarations. And this declaration opens up the possibilities, conversations and actions to make it happen. We always have influence on our future through our choices for our external actions and internal states.
We need to know how we will achieve our future before we can declare our future. Not knowing is a barrier to action ('how' comes before 'what').	We declare our future, and the how discloses itself to us through our practices for exploration, experimentation and design. Dealing with the unknown of the future is a skill that gets developed with practice ('what' comes first and then the 'how').
Action is largely about physical activity.	All action is shaped by language, and the generative acts of language are the actions that shape subsequent actions.

(Continued)

(*Continued*)

Old Interpretation	New Interpretation
Our results come from physical activity (*doing*).	While for certain results, physical activity may be required, all our results have their root cause in conversations—conversations that are had, conversations that are missing, conversations that are performed poorly or conversations that are performed well.
Leaders are people with authority.	We are all leaders. The question is, 'Are we exercising our full-blown leadership in this moment?'

Appendix 2: Form for Declaring a Breakdown and Creating a Future of Design

Area in which you are looking to declare a breakdown (please be as explicit as possible):

_____

_____

_____

Step 1: Declare a Breakdown

Confirm that you are willing to be the cause in the matter of creating a new future in this area of your life. Declare it boldly.

_____

_____

_____

_____

_____

_____

_____

_____

_____

_____

_____

_____

_____

Step 2: Get Present to 'What Is So?'

Get present to the assertions. Be rigorous. Do not allow assessments to be assertions.

Step 3: What Is the Default Future?

If no new action is taken in this area, what is the probable, almost certain future (the default future) in this area? Is this OK with you? Please be rigorous and state explicitly.

Step 4: Create a New Future

Declare a new future in this area. In your declaration, your future gets created and the context for new action emerges.

_____

_____

_____

_____

_____

_____

_____

_____

_____

_____

_____

_____

_____

_____

Step 5: What Is the Missing Action to Go from 'What Is So' to the New Future?

Identify the missing conversational moves—what speech acts, and with whom, will generate actions leading to your declared future.

_____

_____

_____

_____

_____

_____

_____

_____

_____

_____

_____

_____

Step 6: Identify the Execution Steps/Tasks

_____

_____

_____

_____

_____

_____

_____

_____

_____

_____

_____

_____

Appendix 3: Distinctions

Acceptance

- Acceptance is acknowledging *what is*. Acceptance is *not* acknowledging your assessments as 'the truth'.
- Acceptance means that we are centred in the world *as it is* and ready for action, rather than consumed and off-centre with our *assessments or preferences about the situation*.
- We are *present*, and can take action, rather than being in our mood and conversations.
- We are in the mood of 'it is the way it is—now what am I committed to, and what actions will I take to fulfil my commitments?' rather than the mood of 'I don't like the way it is, and I'm going to be triggered and perturbed'.
- Acceptance has a lot to do with letting go.
- Acceptance does not mean agreement or approval.

In committing to the path of mastery in any domain, we can centre ourselves in acceptance by declaring acceptance that 'we are where we are'. We have the skills we have, and do not have the ones we do not have. We learn at the rate we learn, and we do not learn at the rate we do not learn. And it does not have to be any other way, and to insist it should be is to indulge in fantasy. Then, we can accept that we are who we are, and celebrate the gift that this is—that who we are brings the possibilities that we bring.[1]

Action

Action is shaped by language, and the generative acts of language are the actions that shape subsequent actions.

So, in effect:

Action equals generative acts in language, and also physical action that is shaped because of these generative language acts.

We interpret *action* not as some disembodied activity that we have to organize 'out there', but rather as generated by acts of commitments by people who care about some concern.

Action is shaped by commitment—by the commitments we make or do not make, the clarity of the commitment and the ownership and importance of the commitment to the person committing. This is crucial for our understanding of action in organizations, because *the fundamental unit of work in organizations is the agreement*, not the task. Agreements are commitments.

Assertions

An assertion is a claim of fact, which is either true or false, to a standard established by the community.

Assertions can be substantiated or refuted through observation and evidence.

The important elements of assertions are as follows:

- Assertions are claims of facts.
- Assertions are either true or false.
- Assertions are speech acts that are measurable or evidentiary and can be substantiated or refuted through observation and evidence.
- Assertions are to a standard established by the community.

Assessments

An assessment is a statement of evaluation, opinion or judgement. Assessments are neither true nor false. Instead, assessments can be grounded (supported by evidence) or ungrounded.

The important elements of assessments are as follows:

- Assessments are judgements, opinions or conclusions.
- Assessments are never true or false.

- Assessments that you make can open or close possibilities for taking care of a concern.
- Assessments are a speech act and it always has a speaker and a listener (*the speaker and the listener can be the same person when you are having an internal conversation with yourself*).
- Assessments are also most importantly a listening act, and the reason they are called listening acts is because the way you listen to an assessment will impact what action you will take, and hence will impact the result that you have.

Awareness

Awareness means that something has been distinguished in our perceptual field, giving us the potential of paying attention to it and putting it into language. Awareness is the foundation of our power to act and interact with another. To be unaware is to be blind. When we are aware of something, we have a choice in our response to it. When we are unaware, we have no choice.

The realization that awareness is the foundation of all action is behind the principle 'awareness creates choice'. We are literally aware only of what our bodies are trained to be aware of.

Blindness

Blindness is a state where we do not know that we do not know. Blindness is a state of no choice.

Centred

Being centred is being in a physical, mental and emotional state of choice. We are centred when our body, mind and emotions are in a state where we can choose our actions. When we are not in a state to choose our actions, we are 'off-centre'; our reactions and tendencies choose for us. We cannot blend when we are off-centre. In centring, we attain complete balance and focus regardless of our situations.

- Our mind is alert, and we are connected to what we care about and we are free of distracting mental chatter.
- Our mood is serene and open to the current situation.
- Our physical state is dynamically relaxed, alert, balanced around our centre of gravity and ready for action.

These three aspects are mutually connected. We can centre ourselves by starting with any one; the other two will follow. Centring is the skill to put yourself in a state of choice rather than be in reaction when a challenging moment demands your leadership. The centred state is proactive and mindful.

From the body perspective, centre is 2 inches below the belly button.

From the language perspective, centre is silence.

From the emotion perspective, centre is acceptance.

Centring is an embodied commitment to self-knowing.[2]

Conversation

Conversation is the interaction of human beings that creates action, meaning, listening, moods and emotions and the future.

Conversations are not just words, but whole body reactions that are provoked when we interact in language or when we interact and language is provoked.

Conversations include language, moods and emotions, body reactions and experiences and the listening that is based on the history of the people in the conversation. Conversations are shaped in linguistic and cultural practices.[3]

Conversation for Action

We coordinate our actions towards bringing about something specific in the future by clarifying and making certain who is committed to doing what by when. We make promises for specific actions to specific people in specific time frames. We make requests of specific people for specific actions in specific time frames.

The conversation for action involves two parties, the customer and the performer, who work together to negotiate COS to which both will commit. The customer is a person who makes a request, and the performer is the one who makes a commitment. The key milestones in the conversation are as follows:

- *Request*: The customer makes a request along with the COS to the performer.
- *Negotiation*: The performer does one of four things: accepts, declines, counter-offers or commits to commit (defer).
- In the event of a counter-offer that the performer makes to the customer—the customer has the same four choices of accept, decline, counter-offer or commit to commit.
- *Promise*: After the negotiation, the performer makes a promise to perform.
- *Execution*: Performer performs.
- *Declaration of Completion*: Performer declares 'complete' to the customer.
- *Declaration of Satisfaction*: Customer declares satisfaction (or dissatisfaction).
- *Revoke/Cancel*: During this process, the customer can revoke the request, or the performer can cancel the promise.

Conversation for Possibility

Conversations for possibilities shape the way you see the future, and the actions that you take today. Conversations for possibility generate ideas for possible action. This conversation is conducted in a mood of speculation, identifying possible future actions without judging them or committing to them. Its purpose is to generate a range of possible outcomes, especially including many that are not obvious in habitual frameworks and current constraints. To maintain the mood of speculation and generate the richest set of possibilities, the speakers wilfully refrain from making feasibility assessments or commitment. An example is a 'what if' conversation requested by a team member to explore a proposal. Another example is a group brainstorming session that designs goals or ways around obstacles.

The structure for conversations for possibilities includes the following elements:

1. Listen
2. Speculate
3. Choose
4. Declare

Conversations for possibilities culminate with the declaration of a new future of design.

Conversation for Relationship

To get meaningful and productive results with other people, the first conversation you need to have is a *conversation for relationship*. Conversations for relationship create a foundation of workability in which people are free to express their concerns, make open requests and even decline requests. Participants in this conversation relate to each other as a function of their commitments, instead of relating to each other based on the assessments, interpretations and feelings they have about each other. Rather than resigning themselves to patterns of defensive behaviour, resentment or cynicism, they focus on building relationships and opening possibilities through their speaking and listening.

The objective of this conversation is to discover the basis for collaboration between individuals. For the conversation for relationship to be effective, you discover the following in your conversation:

- Shared interest
- Shared care or concern
- Shared commitment

Declaration

A declaration is a speech and a listening act, made by a person of authority to do so, where he or she, out of nothingness, brings forth a new possibility, a new future into existence that they own.

A declaration can begin, resolve or end things.

Default Future

Default future is the future that was going to happen unless something dramatic and unexpected happened. By default future, we do not mean the inevitable future—such as ageing and eventually dying—but rather what is going to happen in our experience, whether we give it much thought or not.[4]

Future of Design

Future of design is the opposite of default future. A future of design is a future you create with your declarations.

Generative Conversations

Communication is considered to describe things, not generate them, to be the transfer of information, with an emphasis on good presentation rather than listening skills. However, language is generative in addition to being descriptive. We focus on the aspects of language and communication that generate action and thereby results; that generate possibilities, meaning, value and satisfaction for ourselves and others; and even generate moods and emotions in our experience.

The relevance of speaking and listening for organizations, leadership and coaching is to recognize the generative power of language. One way that language is understood in our current age is as a description of our world, a set of linguistic tokens for entities in reality, a medium for the transfer of information. Much research in language has worked in this framework—that words correspond to entities and phenomena in the world. We see that a word like 'chair' corresponds to an artefact by that name in the world. As I have said, this perspective hides that *language is generative*, not just descriptive. Language has the power to generate action, the outcomes of action, possibilities, commitment, identities, opinions and much more.

In the 1940s, Oxford philosopher John Austin pointed out that we perform acts in language that are not descriptive, but that generate commitments and the future. He discovered that when we make a promise, for example, we are not describing something in the world. Instead, we are making an act, and the act is one of commitment—showing what the speaker is committed to—for the future. A request is a similar act, in which we do not describe something but rather make an act that shifts the future through the commitment that is spoken, listened and asked for. Austin called these linguistic acts 'speech acts'.[5]

Generative language has the power to create new futures, to craft vision and to eliminate the blinders that are preventing people from seeing possibilities. It does not describe how a situation occurs; it transforms how it occurs. It does this by rewriting the future.[6]

Generative Interpretation

At IGL, we state that for an interpretation to be generative, it must

- be observable,
- be executable,
- be learnable through practice and
- generate the desired result.

Generative Practice

A generative practice is a conscious choice to embody a behaviour that can be used in whatever situation we find ourselves in. It is a commitment to a way of being in the world. It is life affirming, creative, and it produces a reality by how we orient to our life situation.

Learning to type, on the other hand, is a specific practice; it is specific to a certain context and it takes care of a specific concern. But typing is useful only when we are typing. A generative practice we can use anytime, anyplace, even when we are learning to type.[7]

Grounded Assessments

Grounded assessments are assessments that have answered a set of questions that require clarification before the listener can accept the assessment. These questions concern care, standards, domain and evidence.

Grounding is a practice to make assessments about assessments. If an assessment is 'grounded', then it has evidence to an acceptable standard, and is more likely to be effective in producing a desired outcome than an assessment that is 'ungrounded'—lacking clear standards, evidence or specification of the domain of concern. Grounding does not make an assessment true; it only provides evidence and argument that it is a good assessment for our purpose. And ungrounded assessments only mean the assessments lack relevant evidence to trust the assessment. In grounding, we recommend that you ask certain questions.

To ground assessments, we find answers to the following questions:

- For the sake of what future action?
- In which domain of action?
- According to what standard?
- What true assertions support the assessment?
- What true assertions are against the assessment?

So in general, grounding is a way to produce more trust in an assessment.

Internal Conversation

Internal conversation is the conversation that you have with yourself. It is that little voice inside of you that is rarely silent. This internal, little, voice determines how you observe the events in your life.

Interruption

Interruptions are nothing but a break in your transparency. An interruption disrupts the 'established order', and this established order was transparent till the 'interruption' took place.

If something happens that leads us to a different assessment of what it is we can expect in the future, we would call this an interruption. *An interruption implies a change in our space of possibilities.* What we assumed was possible before may no longer be possible or what we assumed may not be possible before may suddenly become a possibility. Whenever the observer assesses the space of possibility has changed, be it in a positive or in a negative way, that observer is facing an interruption.[8]

Leader

A Leader is someone

- who *creates* an extraordinary future, given the perceived current circumstances;
- who gets others to *commit* to this new, extraordinary future; and
- who *takes* and *generates action* to achieve this new future.[9]

Missing Actions

In the world of generative leadership, missing actions are missing conversational moves that are distinguished by the observer. If you do not have the results that you want, there are missing actions/ conversations, those that you need to distinguish first and then have with others and/or with yourself.

Possibility

The common-sense understanding of possibility, as per the *Oxford Dictionaries*, is 'A thing that may happen'.[10] I am not talking about this as possibility that may happen someday in the future.

The possibility that I am talking about in this book is a creation of yours, that empowers you in this moment, shapes the way you think and feel in this moment, to take new action. When you create this kind of a possibility, you impact your 'now'. You impact your present.

For example, when I created the possibility of setting up IGL, India, it changed the way I felt in that moment. I felt a new surge of energy, a new power to take actions that were hitherto unknown to me. A possibility that excites you automatically puts you in the mood for taking action right now. You know you can make this happen, as long as you take actions in line with achieving this possibility.

Presence

To have presence is to *live* in this moment, in the *here* and *now*. Not in your past, and not in your future. To have presence is to be bodily alert in this moment. It is to be aware of your emotional state, its impact on how you see the world and also its impact on others around you.

To have presence is to be connected every moment with the question: 'for the sake of what am I doing what I am doing?' It is being connected to your purpose, and acting in fulfilling your purpose.

The above-mentioned definition is the internal aspect of presence. There is another aspect to presence, which is the external aspect of presence.

Simply put, presence is how you land on others. In others words, presence is the assessment others make of your impact on them. Even before you open your mouth to speak the first word, people may make assessments about you. This assessment is based on the body you show up in and the emotional energy you emit generally, and in particular moments. Of course, once you start to speak, *what* you speak and *how* you speak also impact the way others assess your presence.

The 3 Cs of leadership presence are

- choice,
- care and
- commitment.

Problem

When something happens/does not happen, and for you that should not 'be', then 'it' is a problem. Problems are all about 'what I make of what is so'.

Problems do not exist in reality—they exist in the seeing of the observer.

Relationship

A relationship is a promise.

I am the father of my children. While my children are my own, it is not that because they were born through me that I have a relationship with them of being a father. I am their father because I choose to be in this relationship with them and honour the promise of this relationship. There is a certain set of expectations that my children, my wife, my parents, my children's school and the society have of me as a father. And when I honour their expectations, I do truly become a father in their eyes.

My brother on the other hand has two adopted sons. They were not born through him, and yet, his promise as a father is by no means any less than mine. There are biological fathers, who do not keep the promise of being fathers. So, my claim is that being a father is not about blood, but about a promise.

Similarly, all other relationships are promises. A relationship between a client and the vendor company, a relationship between a subordinate and his line manager, a relationship between a husband and wife and so forth.

Responsibility

Responsibility is being willing to be the cause in the matter. It is taking the posture that you are the source or the cause of something, and that outcomes can be shifted by your actions.

Somatics

The term 'somatics' derives from the Greek word *somatikos*, which signifies the living, aware, bodily person. It posits that neither mind nor body is separate from the other; both being a part of a living process called the soma.

The soma is often referred to as the living body in its wholeness; somatics, then is the art and science of the soma.[11]

Speculation

'A speculation is a conversation in which the participants create new possibilities for future action, and set a context in which those actions make sense.' Speculative conversations relate to what could exist or might be done in the future. The key questions to be asked are 'What is it possible to do?' 'What future would we like to create?' or 'What new can we achieve or create?'[12]

Team

A team is a group of people with a shared promise. A team is constituted in a promise. Without a shared promise, the team is not a team; it is just a group of people together.

Transparency

Transparency is the functioning of a process without the user being aware of its presence.[13]

What Is So?

'What is so?' are assertions, claims of facts, which are either true or false, when compared to a standard established by the community.

What I Make of What Is So?

'What I make of what is so?' are assessments, statements of evaluation, opinion or judgement. Assessments are neither true nor false. Instead, they can be grounded (supported by evidence) or ungrounded.

Notes

1. Dunham in his Leadership papers for the Generative Leadership programme.
2. Richard Strozzi-Heckler, *The Leadership Dojo: Build Your Foundation as an Exemplary Leader* (California: Frog. Ltd, 2007).
3. This distinction of 'conversation' has been created for IGL by Bob Dunham.

4. Steve Zaffron and Dave Logan, *The Three Laws of Performance: Rewriting the future of your organization and your life* (San Francisco: Jossey–Bass/Wiley/ Times Group Books, 2009).
5. Extracted from the papers authored by Robert Dunham, for IGL.
6. Ibid.
7. Ibid.
8. This has been adapted from Rafael Echevarria's (of Newfield Network) paper on 'Moods and Emotions'. While he calls this a break in transparency, I have called this an interruption, as we do at IGL. At Newfield Network, there is no distinction between a break in transparency and a breakdown. At IGL, we distinguish a break in transparency as an interruption, and then based on the observer, she/he may declare a breakdown (or not declare a breakdown).
9. Adapted from the works for Werner Erhard and Michael Jensen.
10. http://www.oxforddictionaries.com/definition/english/possibility?q=Possibility&searchDictCode=all, accessed 18 February 2016.
11. Richard Strozzi-Heckler, *The Art of Somatic Coaching: Embodying Skillful Action, Wisdom, and Compassion* (Berkeley: North Atlantic Books, 2014).
12. Peter J. Denning and Robert Dunham, *The Innovator's Way* (Cambridge: MIT Press, 2010).
13. http://www.oxforddictionaries.com/definition/english/transparent, accessed 18 February 2016.

Index

About the Author

Sameer Dua is committed to transforming lives of people around the world and believes that everyone in this world has a possibility of happiness, success and extraordinary achievement. He empowers people to know what they really love in life and supports them in getting that in their life so that they lead a life full of joy, success and fulfilment.

With over 24 years of experience in management education, Sameer, a master's degree holder, has set up and run institutes in India and London, UK. He had set up an extensive network of education centres in the early 1990s, then unheard of in India. He has worked with programme participants from 52 countries and worked with top-ranked British, American and European universities. Sameer has worked with various national and multinational corporations in training and developing their top/middle-level management as a part of the management programmes delivered by his institution.

Sameer is the Founder Director and Program Leader for IGL, India, which is established in association with IGL, USA. Sameer is a certified trainer from Zig Ziglar Corporation and has conducted many high-quality training programmes and has also successfully coached leaders within organizations to reach their optimum best and achieve their goals. Sameer uses a transformational approach to coaching and training and has undergone an ontological coach training programme from the world's leading ontological coach training institute—The Newfield Network, USA.

Sameer has done several training, coaching and consulting projects with organizations of different industries and varying sizes. Some of his clients include Mercedes-Benz, Siemens, John

Deere, BMC Software, Cosmos Co-operative Bank, Bennett, Coleman and Co. Ltd (The Times of India Group), Allscripts, Persistent Systems, Amdocs, Tech Mahindra, Dana, Cargill, Cognizant, among many others. Sameer gets constant invitations to speak as a keynote speaker, and regularly speaks at business off-sites, industry consortiums and business clubs and was also recently invited to a TEDx talk in Mumbai, India, where he spoke on declaring breakdowns.

Sameer was an advisor to a top-ranked and a leading business school in Asia. Sameer was the Founding Chairman of the Bangalore Chapter of the Higher Education Forum and also the Vice Chairman of the Emerging Presidents' Group.

In accordance with his purpose to positively impact millions of people around the world, Sameer set up the Gift Your Organ Foundation. As the Founder and Chief Catalyst of the Gift Your Organ foundation, Sameer's vision is that there will be no deaths in India for the want of organs. The Gift Your Organ Foundation works with the Karnataka government and the Maharashtra government and is the first organization in the country to have introduced the Green Heart Driver's Licence, which is having an organ donation option on the driver's licence. This one move can potentially transform the entire organ donation landscape in India.

To invite Sameer as a speaker, or to organize a programme on 'declaring breakdowns' in your organization, or for any other queries, you can email him at sameer@sameerdua.com.